GUNS, SNAKES, AND SPIRIT ANIMALS

GUNS, SNAKES, AND SPIRIT ANIMALS
Stories from the Field of Archaeology

POLLY SCHAAFSMA AND MAVIS GREER

SUNSTONE
PRESS

SANTA FE

Sunstone books may be purchased for educational, business, or sales promotional use.
For information please write: Special Markets Department, Sunstone Press,
P.O. Box 2321, Santa Fe, New Mexico 87504-2321.

Design › R. Ahl
Printed on acid-free paper
∞
eBook 978-1-61139-624-9

Library of Congress Cataloging-in-Publication Data

Names: Schaafsma, Polly, author. | Greer, Mavis, author.
Title: Guns, snakes, and spirit animals : stories from the field of
    archaeology / by Polly Schaafsma and Mavis Greer.
Description: Santa Fe, NM : Sunstone Press, [2021] | Summary: "Behind the
    scenes adventures in archaeological field research and travel from the
    American West and Mesoamerica"-- Provided by publisher.
Identifiers: LCCN 2021050037 | ISBN 9781632933294 (paperback) | ISBN
    9781611396249 (epub) | ISBN 1632933292 (paperback)
Subjects: LCSH: Archaeologists--Anecdotes. |
    Archaeology--Fieldwork--Anecdotes.
Classification: LCC CC175 .S33 2021 | DDC 930.1--dc23/eng/20211108
LC record available at https://lccn.loc.gov/2021050037

WWW.SUNSTONEPRESS.COM
SUNSTONE PRESS / POST OFFICE BOX 2321 / SANTA FE, NM 87504-2321 /USA
(505) 988-4418

DEDICATION

To all the unknowing participants in these stories.

CONTENTS

INTRODUCTION
by
POLLY SCHAAFSMA AND MAVIS GREER

Untold tales lurk behind all those volumes—the books and reports of archaeological information stored in libraries, residing on the shelves of archaeologists' offices, or squirreled away in digital mode. Behind the formal, structured content of archaeological literature with its descriptions of field work and information gathering and the resulting data that are subsequently subjected to anthropological models and theorizing, supported by charts and scientific syntheses, are hidden the real life experiences of the archaeologist, including adventurous events that enveloped his or her research leading to a publication. The absence of such peripheral incidents, and therefore distractions is, of course, essential. While these personal stories are sometimes shared between archaeologists over a beer, at parties, conferences, or a dinner, they are seldom written down. Here we endeavor to tell a few of those stories.

Archaeologists face many challenges in their efforts to understand the past. As hard as it is to believe for those of us dedicated to this quest, there are actually those in our very own society—huge blocks of people, as a matter of fact—that lack any interest in and appreciation whatsoever for archaeology. Those groups commonly include pot-hunters, land developers, miners, fossil fuel companies, and so forth, and if archaeological sites harboring information of the ancient cultural history of this continent stand in the way of any moneyed interests, there is a conflict of values. While laws exist to negotiate these differences, the archaeologist, even with legal protection, may find him or herself directly confronting a belligerent adversary. And then there are territorial issues where the land 'overseers' feel threatened by the mere presence of an archaeologist. These land proprietors include rattlesnakes, ranchers, and indigenous stakeholders who may or may not hold exclusive rights to land and places of interest to the archaeologists who are legally mandated to carry out investigations within their boundaries. In these situations, misunderstandings are apt to run rampant, and guns are likely to be drawn as described herein.

Another problem with "space-sharing," you might call it, is when being in the wrong place at the wrong time gets dangerous. A couple of incidents related here describe unpredictable and unexpected encounters when the search for a site involved running into the business end of a drug deal—once in isolated mesquite bushes along the American/Mexican border and in another time and place, a close call in a Mexican border village.

In writing and assembling these stories we found they not only have entertainment value but they also have teaching value as well. Some are cast in the historical context of the times specifically, the late 1960s, the mood of which sheds a distinctive light on the 'social complexity' and the ensuing difficulties of field expeditions. Other narratives are concerned with vast differences in how rock art is interpreted. Persisting over centuries, even millennia, petroglyphs and rock paintings are the object of countless fantasies; interpretations stick like Velcro once the story is deemed good enough. Like a Rorschach test, responses to ancient imagery are elicited in accordance with the programing of the observer—some popular interpretations include the ideas that petroglyphs were made by aliens, angels, the little people, or a 'race' lost such as ancient European explorers—such explanations are not uncommon. Wild and woolly stories, laced with imaginative meanings and impossible origins, test the patience of any researcher. While humbly recognizing our own limitations in the interpretive business, we archaeologists can at least "corral the territory" within which reasonable interpretations may reside. On a humanistic note, the reflective accounts of the Spirit Deer and the Water Serpent are included to show how engagement with natural elements, enhanced by native perspectives and metaphors of understanding, may enrich one's experiences and perceptions.

Finally, some stories are included for their historical value in order to correct misconceptions passed on within only a few decades about evidence of vandalism and other events that have taken place at rock art sites. These include the gouged cliff face in the Dinetah in northwestern New Mexico with rock art missing, and the painting of a rock art panel with old-style images to promote tourism at a cave along the Rocky Mountain front in Montana. When referring to specific sites we often call them by name, but sites sometimes are known by several different names so in order to assure archaeologists are on the same page a numbering system for sites was developed by the Smithsonian in the 1930s and 40s consisting of the state number, county abbreviation, and sequential site number, such as 24FR2.

And on another final note, dear reader, you will notice that some of these accounts are accompanied by photographs, and for others there are none at all. These differences relate to the archival resources of the writers, what has been saved, and whether or not any photos were even taken. We particularly regret most of all that none of the tense moments described in this book were conducive to picture-taking. All photos that are included were taken by Curt or Polly Schaafsma or John or Mavis Greer unless otherwise credited. Photos were prepared for publication by John.

For the most part in the following stories the names of the participants are included. Our husbands, Curt Schaafsma and John Greer, and our sons, Hoski and Pieter Schaafsma and Brian Greer, are often mentioned as they were integral parts of these adventures. In some cases we simply cannot remember the name of the person involved, we never knew their name, or it's better not to mention it, but if a name is essential to the story, we give the person one and let you know it's a pseudonym. Though archaeologists study people that are long gone, the study of the past involves interacting with the living as these stories demonstrate. We are not Indiana Jones action swashbucklers, but we are also not loners holed up in a dark laboratory, wrapped up in dusty artifacts with no live interaction. Instead we are somewhere in between supporting the dream of the many people who respond to us when we tell them what we do with "I always wanted to be an archaeologist."

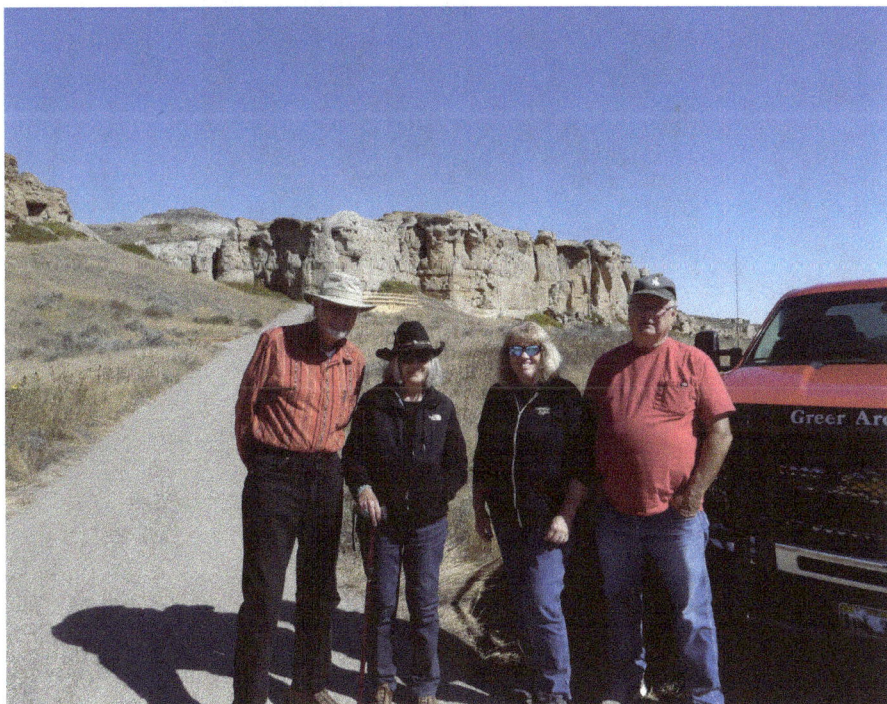

Curt, Polly, Mavis, and John at Writing-on-Stone Provincial Park, Alberta, Canada, 2018. (Photograph by a park guide)

1

GUNS AND OTHER SCARY MOMENTS

Historic rock paintings of guns shooting and tally marks.
Pictograph Cave, 24YL1, Montana. (Photograph by John Greer)

RIFLES IN EVERY PICKUP
by
POLLY SCHAAFSMA

"There he is!" A woman in the crowd yells out tugging at her friend's sleeve while gleefully pointing at Curt as we descend the stairs of the Catron County courthouse. We are leaving the courtroom with a huge throng of locals on the way to lunch at the only eatery in town right across the street. Then someone else throws a taunt. As they leave the building throwing jibes, we pause by the door at the bottom of the stairs in front of the candy and fast food dispenser, having second thoughts about the restaurant where everyone is headed. It is suddenly apparent that over there we will be surrounded by a rowdy, hostile bunch of folks that is not above provocation. The paired, saloon-styled swinging doors at the entrance seem to issue a visual warning. For us, lunch that day will be the delightful choices offered by the handy dandy candy machine we are looking at. Our only ally in the building is a State Attorney from Santa Fe, and she joins us for cheese and crackers and chocolate bars, the best junk food in town.

It is the early summer of 1979, and we are in Reserve, New Mexico for a hearing. Curt, the newly installed State Archaeologist, has busted a pot-hunter who was illegally digging through an archaeological site with a bulldozer, and we are here for a trial. I'm just along for the ride. It is against state law to 'excavate' archaeological sites with machinery on any kind of property, including private land, and this guy has been out there on a ranch with a big-time machine crashing around looking for pots to sell on the black market. Curt is armed with official papers describing the crime, the written testimony bolstered with numerous black and white photographs that Curt himself took on a former trip when he was able to document the devastation in progress. Locally this type of activity is regarded as "private enterprise," however, to be lauded and defended under any circumstances. Having driven down from Santa Fe early that morning in a white sedan with the State of New Mexico seal emblazoned on the door, upon our arrival we feel, to say the least, conspicuous and uncomfortable. The streets of Reserve are packed tight with pickup trucks, each with a rifle or two on display across the back window.

Inside, the courthouse is packed with ranchers and other local folks attending on behalf of their pot-hunting friend. An individualistic ideology asserting unfettered rights to do anything you want to do, including the right to destroy archaeological sites in a quest for saleable artifacts, is a stance staunchly defended by ranchers throughout the West. And we know in advance that the folks in Catron County are a particularly tough bunch. About ten years earlier a rancher, who had kindly taken us to rock art on his property, had entertained us at his kitchen table with tales of the early settlers of the region—his own family included—that were escapees from the law, due to troubles they had gotten into in the East and Midwest. Catron County was a good place to hide and everyone was still proud of their heritage and acting accordingly. So here we are—representatives of the law—them against us.

In the courtroom, an overweight judge, who seems particularly overbearing in his floppy black robe, is trying to round up a jury from the rather raucous bunch of people gathered there. So far every interviewee for this position has exuberantly and proudly proclaimed support for the pothunter. The difficult endeavor of finding unbiased recruits, is compounded by the amusing problem that the "Honorable Judge Mitchell" is having a very hard time pronouncing "archaeology." He stumbles on the 'ch' through the morning until lunchtime when the bunch leaves en masse for lunch across the street behind the swinging doors.

Nothing was ever "accomplished" that day, or ever. No jury, no trial. The judge tried the jolly strategy of referring to the pothunter and perpetrator of the crime, as Curt's colleague, in an effort to "buddy them up." They were both interested in archaeology after all. The case was dissolved, but I can't recall the grounds for this.

The air is still tense in the late afternoon when we leave the courthouse. As hungry as we are by now, we decide that the local restaurant is still a bad, even dangerous, choice. Back on the street in our brilliantly white car, we can't wait to get out of town. We feel like a blazing target. The nearest place to eat on the way is Datil—also a small town with a single restaurant. Still uncomfortable, 67 miles from Reserve still feels too close and it is likely that ranchers from there were among the crowd. We drive another 60 or so more miles to Socorro that night before eating.

GUN TOTING LANDOWNERS
by
MAVIS GREER

Guns are common in Wyoming and Montana, and in many field situations we carry a gun to shoot snakes or deer hit on the highway. However, we're not the only ones with guns, and in some instances we've been on the wrong end of them.

It was the summer of 1975 and my first summer in the field. Floyd Sharrock, who was the head of the University of Montana Statewide Archaeological Survey at that time, sent Lisa, Carl, Chuck, and me to far northwestern Montana to do a survey near Kootenai Falls for the Forest Service as part of their obligations to find, record, and manage the archaeological sites on their lands. This heavily timbered area with tall fir, spruce, and pine trees had few roads then, so in order to shorten our hiking time to the survey area and to have more time for actually working we decided to see if we could cross a short piece of private land that would quickly get us to where we needed to be. We drove up the two-track through the dense forest and parked our pickup at the end of the landowner's driveway in an area hidden from the house by a slope, a slight bend, and, of course, dense timber. Lisa, who was in charge of our crew, and I walked up the driveway to talk with the landowner, leaving the two guys in the pickup. The house was a small, almost cabin-like structure typical of a hermit hide-away in the woods. There were flowers blooming around the house, but they looked more like accidental happenings rather than a planned garden. As we approached the house we were greeted by a short, older man holding a long rifle pointed at us standing in front of his house. I'm not sure how he knew we were coming to his door unless he was watching his driveway constantly as we made a quiet approach. However, by then it was too late to retreat back down the driveway, so we began explaining that we wanted to cross his property to get to Forest Service land where our project was located. He didn't seem to be completely there mentally (shades of the movie *Deliverance*), but he was well aware he had a captive audience.

As he stood there holding the gun in our general direction, he began to talk about people trespassing, problems with the government, and where we wanted to go, but in the midst of these topics he would change the subject to his "posies." During some of these rants he waved his gun around and at times forgot to point it at us and let it point at the ground. He told us how well his posies were doing this season and wanted to make sure that we looked at them, which we obediently did praising their beauty. Lisa and I exchanged many looks and individually tried to think of ways to get out of there without upsetting him further. We finally just started walking back down the driveway while at the same time telling him that we would find a different way into the survey area. He did not want to let us go and followed us down the driveway continuing to talk about his favorite subjects, which of course included the posies, and he was still holding his gun, which he occasionally pointed at us. Once we rounded the slight bend and he saw that there were two men with us, his anger flared, and he started addressing the two guys, who were sitting in the back of the pickup waiting for us.

"What? You sent the women up to sweet talk me into letting you onto my property?" At that point we thought he really might use the gun, but not on Lisa and me. By then he was ready to shoot the guys, so we hustled into the pickup and sped down the road leaving him and his gun at the end of his driveway.

Years later John and I returned to that area to visit some sites. We took the long way in right from the start, although it is doubtful that the man with the gun was still among the living.

As a side note, to cross the Kootenai River at the falls, it is necessary to walk on a swinging bridge. I had told John many stories about the bridge and how scary it was. To my (and his) disappointment when we got to the bridge in 1996 the old one from the 1970s had been replaced by a new, sturdy, suspension bridge that hardly moved at all.

About eight years later I was again on the wrong end of a gun. This time John and I and Brian, who was about 3 years old at the time, were in northeastern Wyoming, on our way to do an archaeological survey of a well pad prior to its construction. The well pad was to be built and drilled on private surface, but because the minerals were owned by the federal government the oil company needed an archaeologist to inventory the area they were going to disturb, record any archaeological sites we found there, and write a report in order for the company to get their permit. In the early 1980s we trusted the oil company we were doing the survey for to contact the ranchers and let them know we were going to be on their property. However, after being burned on that several times, such as what happened on this day, we now make a practice of contacting the landowners ourselves.

Thinking we had permission to be at the planned well pad, we left Interstate 90 and headed north on a gravel road through the sage-covered countryside among the red, scoria-capped knolls on a nice summer day. Turning off the county road onto a two-track we were driving through a pasture to the staked well pad when two men (the rancher and his grown son) drove up in an old pickup from the opposite direction. We stopped, and they pulled up next to us so the drivers doors were next to one another. Both men got out with the father aiming a pistol at us. They wanted to know what we were doing there, and John got out to let them know that we were there to do the archaeology on the staked well pad in their pasture and that the company said we had permission.

Well, we don't know if the company told them or not as they were not in the mood to let us know what they knew. They just wanted us to leave, but at the same time they were keeping us there by pointing a gun at us and not letting us move. Naively we thought by explaining why we were there it would change their minds and they would let us go ahead and do the survey. However, they would have none of that, and then it came down to trying to reason with them as to why they should let us leave. They finally decided that since we had a small child with us, we could go, and we quickly did with them watching to make sure we drove off their property.

TERROR AT TOQUIMA CAVE
by
POLLY SCHAAFSMA

"My name's Bob," he says.

It is a clear, cool, late spring day, and we've been driving east through central Nevada along Route 50, known as the West's loneliest road. We're on our way home to New Mexico following a rock art conference near Reno, and after spending the night in Austin, Nevada, we decide to take a 30 mile side trip on a dirt road to Toquima Cave, known for its paintings and prehistoric ritual significance. The dirt road is narrow and also little traveled, and we never encounter another car.

Toquima Cave, managed by the US Forest Service, is just off the road, and about a quarter of a mile from the cave is a small parking area where we leave our car. The walk to the cave takes us along a lovely forested trail, lined with wildflowers, the air pungent with pine. The 'cave' is located along a slope. It is really a rock shelter open to the south, and today it is closed off by a metal fence beyond which the paintings are visible. The shelter is rather small, the distances not great between the protective fence and the paintings. We understand that the local Native Americans still regard it as a sacred place.

It is isolated, lonely, and quiet. No sounds but bird calls, the rustle of leaves moved by a slight breeze. We take our time photographing the multi-colored designs through the openings in the grid. I am finished taking pictures and am putting away my camera, when suddenly we hear heavy footprints moving toward us through the thick brush below the cave, a direction different from the official trail we had taken. A large, rather husky, Euro-American man emerges. He is middle-aged, wearing jeans and a plaid shirt. He offers a brief introduction, but little more is said, except that he adds that he is surprised to find anyone here. He shows little interest in the paintings, and we privately wonder what brought him here. Was it the mere fact that the cave is visible from the road below and he thought he'd check it out. Or something else? Ready to leave, we have been enjoying the solitude and are not really interested in engaging in conversation with this guy. He climbs up to the fence and sits down with his back to the cave, positioning himself above us, where he psychologically dominates the entire scene. I adjust my pack and prepare to leave.

"You guys have no fear," he says.

I'm starting to walk away. My immediate intuition is that if we engage in conversation, he will manipulate it to cause a confrontation.

"Fear of what?" Curt responds, after several seconds of dead silence.

"Violent crime," he answers.

Panicked, heart racing, I'm walking away fast, my back toward him, resisting the urge to run. I expect to be shot.

"Well, I guess if you have no fear" he continues, "Nothing will happen to you."

No fear? I am terrified! Curt is walking behind me now, and we disappear down the trail, into the woods. Who is he? Will he follow us? Is he armed? We reach our car and leave, but my panic does not go away. For the next 30 miles to the highway I worry. Might he have driven ahead somehow and blocked the narrow dirt road...what if...what if...

The horror of the situation stayed with me. It was a month before I gathered the courage to call the Forest Service to ask if there had been any 'incidents' at Toquima Cave. Their response was—as one would expect—negative.

TRAVEL ANTIDOTES FROM SOUTH OF THE BORDER

by

Mavis Greer

We have had the opportunity to travel extensively across the world, and there are lots of small incidents that stand out. Two in 1983 are especially memorable.

On Brian's third birthday we went to Guatemala to see Tikal and Quiriguá. It turned out we had some extra time, so we decided to go to Honduras to see the site of Copán. We headed for the border crossing just north of Copán in our small rental car. The border station there was just a small building along a dirt road with a barrier across the road and a couple of people on watch. At the border they wouldn't let us cross with the rental car, which was really disappointing to be so close and yet so far. However, after talking with the border patrol agent for a short while he saw an opportunity to make some money while at the same time fulfilling our desire to see the site. He had us park the rental on the Guatemalan side of the border and walk across as he had a friend who would drive us to the site and back. He assured us our vehicle would be safe with him, and we didn't doubt it at this back woods crossing. Very shortly his friend showed up in a small pickup, the kind that was very popular in the late seventies and early eighties. We piled into the small cab, the friend driving, me in the middle with my legs trying to stay away from the floor shift, and John on the end with Brian on his lap, and off we went down the curving mountain road to Copán. Once in those close quarters, we soon realized our driver had been taken away from an afternoon of drinking, which was scary enough, but on top of that we were driving down a narrow, very curvy, dirt mountain road. At each curve he loudly honked his horn to warn anyone coming from the opposite direction that we were there, but it is unlikely that should someone have been there we could have stopped or squeezed by them. As we're on this terrifying roller coaster ride, our driver is talking non-stop, mostly about papas. Not thinking too clearly, we thought he was talking about potatoes, but the context was quite bizarre as it was one of visitation. However, as we entered town by the site it all made sense as there were many signs advertising the Pope was coming to visit.

At the site he let us out at the entrance. As we're getting out he yells, "I'll be back in a couple of hours. In the meantime, if you need me, I'll be at the bar down the street." Wow, that made us feel so much better about our return trip up the mountain. As we walked out of the site in a couple of hours there he was and was just as animated or more so going back to the border having imbibed the entire time we were at the site. It was such a relief to see our vehicle and to get in for a slow, boring ride through the Guatemalan jungle.

In that same year we made a quick trip to Belize to visit a Mayan site Dr. Richard "Scotty" MacNeish was excavating and another being excavated by Drs. Tom Hester and Harry Shafer. We flew into Belize City and were given an old 4x4 Toyota at the rental place, which we thought would be fine for our short trip. We were then off to visit Scotty's site. At that time he was working in coastal Belize on open-air sites, which was something different for this archaeologist famous for excavating dry caves. Scotty gave us a great tour of the site, and to our surprise one of the people we saw in the lab was another Wyoming archaeologist. Scotty was a detailed tour guide, and he introduced us to each crew chief as we went from one excavation unit to the next. At one point a young crew chief said something about our credentials and Scotty explained to him in no uncertain terms that we were experienced archaeologists and running a contract business in Wyoming. We were surprised how much he knew about us and even more surprised that he would defend us to a cocky young crew chief.

We left the site as it was getting dark and soon it was raining. We found the old truck had no heater and we were dressed for hot Belize, not cold Belize, plus we had a three-year old who was getting cold and tired. We were not prepared to spend the night in the truck as we were traveling with a small carry-on since we only planned to be there for a couple of days. We had nothing to cover up with and knew we had to find someplace to spend the night. We were so happy to arrive in Orange Walk, Belize. We were sure we could get a motel room, even though it was getting late. We finally found a place that looked like it had a vacancy, and John went to find someone to rent us a room. It was not long and he was back at the truck with directions to a room in a nearby building. We gathered our meager belongings and went in. As we entered we thought the place looked abandoned, but we couldn't be choosey at that point. Finding our room, we entered and found two beds with sheets on them (no blankets or pillows), a single light bulb hanging from the ceiling, and a toilet on what can only be described as a small stage. It was positioned on a raised area above the floor with the beds and was completely open to the small room. It was quite out of the ordinary, but it was out of the rain, so we were happy campers. The next morning, with better light we soon discovered our thoughts about abandonment were right on. That place hadn't been operational in years, but we were happy the owner took pity on us and let us get out of the rain. However, Brian didn't fare as well as we did. He woke up covered with welts from bed bugs.

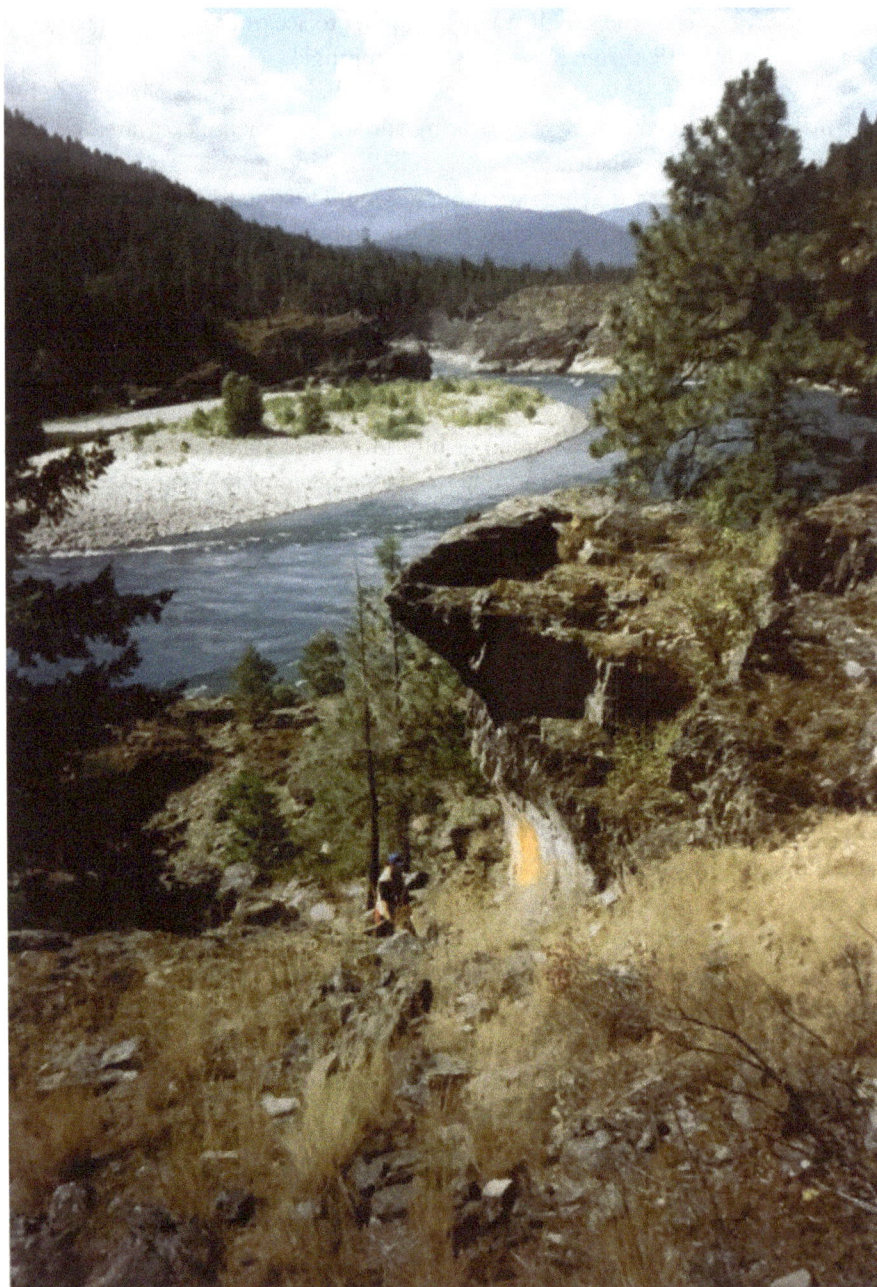

Kootenai River below the falls. John in front of a rock art site.
(Photograph by Mavis Greer)

New suspension bridge across the Kootenai River. (Photograph by John Greer)

Mavis standing by well pad centerstakes. (Photograph by John Greer)

View of landscape from Toquima Cave, Nevada. (Photograph by Curt Schaafsma)

Toquima Cave with metal barrier. (Photograph by Curt Schaafsma)

Painted polychrome abstract elements as seen through the grid.
(Photograph by Polly Schaafsma)

Mavis and Brian at Quiriguá, Guatemala.
(Photograph by John Greer)

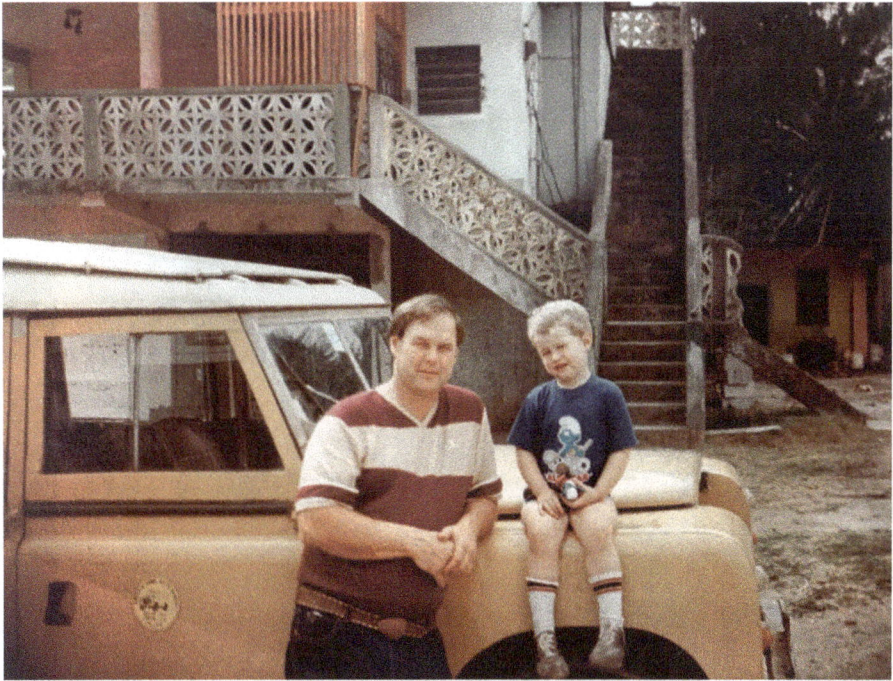

John and Brian with 4x4 in Belize.
(Photograph by Mavis Greer)

2
SNAKES

CM Russell Boulder, 24CA623, Montana.
(Photograph by John Greer)

IT DOESN'T PAY TO BE A SNAKE AROUND AN ARCHAEOLOGIST

by

Mavis Greer

Even though snakes are common around rock art sites in most areas, and rattlesnakes are often seen at archaeological sites on the Plains and in the Southwest, people leading tours feel obligated to warn everyone to watch for snakes before any excursion. This warning often irritates me, and my thoughts go to "does this tour leader think I am an inexperienced site visitor or just stupid." I hate snakes, so I would never get that close to a snake of any kind on purpose, would quickly get out of its way if I see it, and never mess with a rattler. After those initial thoughts, my mind goes to some of my snake experiences, and I realize warnings are probably necessary for some people, although they're often not heeded by anyone.

In the summer of 1976 I floated the Smith River in central Montana for the first time of what would turn out to be several times. The Smith River is a north-flowing tributary to the Missouri, which runs into that river just southwest of Great Falls, Montana. Today this is a popular fly-fishing river, and you have to apply for a permit way in advance to float. The permit also assigns you places to camp, which have rocks for campfires and outdoor toilets that are open to the countryside so from some of them you can watch floaters and fisherman below you as you do your business.

In 1976 the Smith was basically unknown to the outside world, and pre-arrangement weren't needed for floating or camping. That summer I was working for the Lewis & Clark National Forest as their first ever archaeologist. It was also my first archaeological job on my own, so we were learning the ropes together. At this time those in management positions on the Forest could see that things were changing and the river would soon be overrun with people looking for the wilderness floating and fishing experience. The previous summer two archaeologists, Jim Keyser and Audrey Murray, had floated the river on their own and found and recorded several rock art sites, so Floyd Sharrock (who was at this time the Region 1 Forest Archaeologist) decided we should float the river in advance of formal camping developments to look for and record archaeological sites. Therefore, three of us put in the river at Camp Baker to spend five days floating to the take out point at Eden Bridge. Sharrock and I were there to do archaeology, and a guy from the Forest Service, Buzz, was there to paddle the rafts and get us safely down the river. Half way through the trip, the Forest Service sent a helicopter to resupply us with food and to replace Buzz with another support person. When they radioed us to see what supplies we needed them to bring, the only thing we could think of was Diet Pepsi, which they brought to us with no questions asked.

Our days were spent stopping to survey along the river to look for tipi rings, artifacts, and especially rock art sites and then recording those sites. The guys along to paddle the raft, however, were often bored during the day. Buzz was a constant joker and loved to try and freak out the only female on the trip. I thought I was getting used to his shenanigans when one day during a stop to check out a bluff for rock art he found a snake near the river. I was on a slope about 30 feet above him when he wound up and tossed the snake toward me. Luckily, I was holding a long stick, and I stuck it out and caught the snake around it in midair. Because it was still in motion, the snake boomeranged back toward him near the river. It was one of the best catches I've ever made, although the poor snake was undoubtedly traumatized, although not otherwise hurt. The look on Buzz's face was priceless.

In the early 1970s several archaeologists were heading to the Little Rocky Mountains in northeastern Montana for a weekend of camping. I was driving my little black Ford car known affectionately as "The Black Beauty." We were car pooling to save on gas, and one of the people riding with me was a girl I just met when she got into my car. On the highway not far out of Lewistown, Montana, we saw a rattlesnake on the road. She became overjoyed and insisted we stop the car. The snake was already dead from a previous driver, so I was not too concerned (did I mention, I hate snakes?). She jumped out of the car and ran to check out the snake. The rest of us thought she was going to cut off the rattlers for a souvenir, but instead she runs back to the car and finds a plastic bag and puts the entire snake in it. The rest of us did not want that snake anywhere in the car, including the trunk. However, in the end we relented and let her bring it with us as long as she kept it by her feet and took it out of the car as soon as we got to the campsite, which she did. At the campsite she hung the snake from a tree branch and proceeded to skin it to make a hatband. I must admit I prefer to ride in a car with a snake hatband rather than a dead (hopefully) rattler in a plastic bag.

In the mid 1980s John and I were testing a site south of Casper in central Wyoming. The site was close to home so every night we'd pack up and drive across several ground-level bedrock exposures with intervening areas of sand to get to the two-track that led to the county road and then home. One day a rattlesnake visited us at the site, and John killed it since we were returning there every day with Brian, who was about 8 years old at the time, and we didn't want to be surprised by that snake again. After killing the rattler, he put a pinflag through the snake, which was on a sandy patch on the sandstone bedrock, so we could easily see where it was. The next morning we returned to find no sign of the snake—no skin, no pieces, nothing. However, the pinflag was still in place—not tipped over, not bent, but with the red flag still waving proudly in the Wyoming wind. A good meal was provided for some tidy animal that night.

Along the Rocky Mountain front in central Montana we have recorded several rock art sites in limestone rockshelters that are homes to rattlesnakes. One hot summer day we went to a nice shelter along the Dearborn River. The site is on private land, and after stopping by the ranch house and talking to the woman who owned it, we continued on our way across grassy fields to the rock outcroppings along the river. We quickly saw this was a rattlesnake den, and as we entered the rockshelter three rattlers stretched out on the limestone floor began to move. Two snakes immediately dived for a crack along the back wall placing them out of sight and out of harms way (both for them and for us). The third rattler, however, was going to stand his ground and not let us into the shelter. Since this was the only day we had permission to be at the site, we were not going to let a snake deter us from recording, and John proceeded to send the snake to the spirit world. When we left the site for the day, we stopped at the ranch house to tell the woman that we were leaving. We let her know that we had killed a rattler, and she was quite pleased. She told us she shot all rattlers she encountered on the ranch. John asked her if she used a 22. She told him, "Hell no, I use a twelve-gage!"

Usually we see one rattler at a time, but there's a place north of Interstate 90 not far northwest of Sheridan, Wyoming, and the Tongue River where rattlesnakes gather in what cannot be viewed as anything but a herd. One summer day John, Brian, and I left the interstate and traveled north on the improved gravel road through an old gravel pit area to our survey area. After a long day of survey, we were heading back to Sheridan at dusk and driving slowly through the old gravel pit area admiring the setting sun over the Bighorn Mountains in the distance when we started to see snakes in the road. As we got closer we saw many, many snakes in the road. After we had passed through the area in the morning, rattlers had stretched out on the warm gravel road during the day and were now starting to move off as evening approached. We had never seen so many rattlers in one place and were so happy to be in the pickup and not out walking. From that point on we referred to this road as Rattlesnake Alley and never fail to talk about it as we drive north from Sheridan on I-90. Although we didn't intentionally kill any of these snakes, we undoubtedly ran over a few. This is a great source area for those who want snakeskins for hatbands or rattlers for their collection.

SNAKE ETIQUETTE
by
POLLY SCHAAFSMA

It's a fact that snakes and archaeologists tend to frequent the same places—for quite different reasons, of course. The snakes feel cozy in their homes snugged away behind boulders or hidden in the depths of caves. Rock art doesn't concern them much. But those same labyrinths of cliffs and boulders with petroglyphs and rock paintings will also pull the curious humans into the snakes' residential spaces. Although noisy archaeologists or tourists visiting these serpentine neighborhoods usually keep the occupants in retreat, we have also learned to exercise caution when prowling around—rattlesnakes in particular become really irritated by human intruders that are prone to thoughtlessly interrupting their sunbathing on a nice warm rock covered with petroglyphs.

Here in the Southwest we also know that snakes just love to inhabit the cracks and crannies of those stone walls of rooms, now left in quiet loneliness, as their builders moved on centuries ago. On an August afternoon at one of these places now surrounded in solitude, four of us are looking over an early 18th century Navajo pueblito in New Mexico. Many of the masonry walls are still standing, and in a lower room fronted by an open courtyard, several old-style Spanish hooded fireplaces remain remarkably intact. I am very excited to get photographs. These are the finest examples of these fragile structures I've ever seen.

Without giving it a thought, with camera in hand, I hop down into the lush green vegetation growing in the enclosure. Immediately I hear the familiar sizzle of rattlesnakes. They seem to be everywhere—all around—I am surrounded. The grass is tall and I see them slithering and green like the grass, on both sides of me. "Snakes!" I yell. Curt comes running and from above yanks me out of there by one arm, and I am up and safe. Looking down I watch two frightened Prairie Rattlers skedaddling as fast as they can go toward the safety of the old walls. All three of us are terrified of each other—and with good reason. But now I feel kind of bad—I had no business there—at least without knocking. Next time I'll toss in a rock or two to announce myself and politely wait for anyone around to respond.

Dr. Floyd Sharrock and Mavis along Smith River, 1976.
(Photograph by traveling companion)

Helicopter bringing new paddler and supplies. (Photograph by Mavis Greer)

A rattlesnake hides under a ledge at Legend Rock (48HO4), Wyoming.
(Photograph by Mavis Greer)

The Black Beauty ready for a road trip outside of Ronan, Montana.
(Photograph by Mavis Greer)

Mavis at the Lookout Cave (24PH402) entrance in the Little Rockies, northeastern Montana. (Photograph by John Greer)

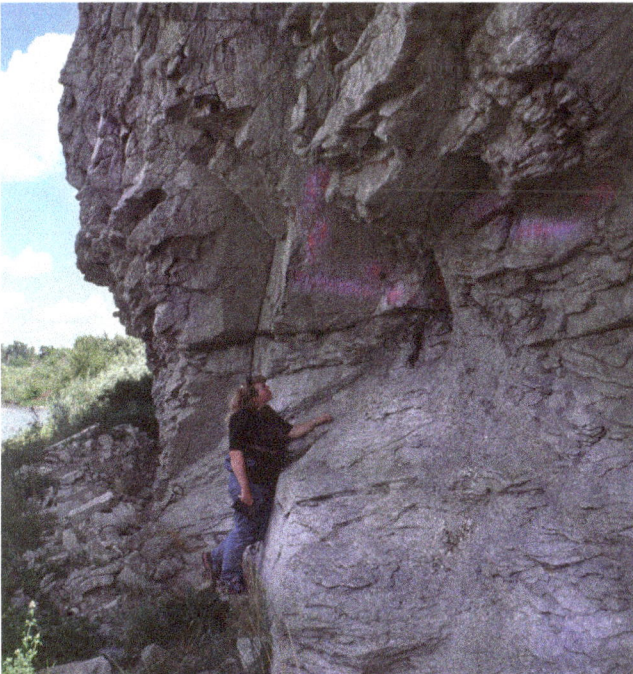

Mavis standing beside the rock art at the Dearborn Confluence site (24LC35), central Montana. Just minutes before this photo was taken there were three rattlesnakes at the base of the cliff. (Photograph by John Greer)

Polly at snake-infested 18th century Navajo pueblito in New Mexico.
(Photograph by Curt Schaafsma)

3
SPIRITUALITY

Owls and other typical images at the Dinwoody type site (48FR109), west-central Wyoming.
(Photograph by John Greer)

THE GREAT WATER SERPENT VISITED THIS YEAR, AND IT WAS NO SMALL EVENT

by

POLLY SCHAAFSMA

His picture is all around, of course, so he is no stranger to those of us who live here. Ancestors of the Pueblo people made his image on rocks everywhere in the Galisteo Basin where we live and beyond, south all the way to Chihuahua. These pictures are often large, and he wears a big horn on this head, a checkered collar representing corn, and sometimes he has a cloud on his tail. In one of these petroglyphs, he is upside down, and a corn plant sprouts upward from his mouth. He is said to bring wind, rain, and storms, floods and earthquakes. In some renderings he is associated with the Morning Star related to war—conflict that resulted in trophy scalps, that were magically transformed into rain-bringers, thus ensuring the victors of an ample supply of corn. Native oral traditions elaborate this serpent's awesome and sometimes punishing nature that inspires fear. I once wrote a paper in which I described his character as fraught with change, destruction, and uncertainty. So while he is no stranger, an actual rare appearance is not to be taken lightly.

July. It is another hot, dry, mid-summer afternoon. We have given up any hope of rain again this year, and the land is bleak. Trees lining the arroyo in our backyard outside our kitchen window are mostly dead or have not leafed out. The earth is pale and parched, and we are grateful for five minute showers that have been the defining events of our recent "rainy seasons." Nothing much. The same again today with a few clouds, although the sky is dark toward the mountains. I retreat into our cool, rock room for a nap. Maybe the rumble of thunder in the east will lull me into dozing. Sleep would be nice, since this heat is tiring.

I lie there listening for a while, hopeful. The thunder is incessant, but it will not rain here because rains don't come from that direction. But what is that swishing noise—the wind maybe, or something else—could it be rain after all? The dogs bark, Curt yells. I hasten.

Roaring past our windows the convulsing shiny streak of the Great Water

Serpent, reflecting silver under a partly cloudy sky, has flooded our arroyo, leveling the landscape. It is bigger than the Rio Grande and fierce.

Outside, a closer look reveals a thick brown water body humped up and bursting over the arroyo banks carrying on its glittery back everything it can steal in its frenzied path—whole trees with roots in the air, tires, boards and plywood, fragments of a corral, a kaleidoscope of bright plastics. A full-sized propane tank bounces merrily, seemingly happy with the ride to nowhere.

We stand back and photograph the raucous scene. It goes on for hours, this relentless serpent of water until it gradually dwindles, eventually vanishing. Sinking into the sands it has delivered, this once demonic power now turned cowardly prankster, has gone into hiding. No culprit to be found. I thought I could hear it laughing.

We walk along its path with newly exaggerated bends, side-stepping now quiet pools and fresh quicksand, fascinated by the elegant patterns of exposed roots, the newly delivered chunks of bright pink mountain granite, and crisply sculpted sandbars. Caught above our heads in branches of trees bent by the flood, is another story—great dark messy tangles of plant debris—and even rocks— mixed with all manner of junk. Strewn everywhere are tires, boards, bottles and other colorful plastics, ropes, wires, cement blocks, ponderosa blocks of someone's now scattered pile of firewood—stuff that the water snake tired of carrying, and dropped in its waning moments. The familiar waterfall formed by a natural rock dam across the arroyo is now twice as high, and the Water Serpent's belly dislodged boulders and scoured down to rough bedrock the once sandy channel below. We begin to collect the litter that we can disentangle or even carry. The rusted fragment of an old garden rake reminds me of the rain symbolism found in petroglyphs, and I take it home to hang in my kitchen.

True to character as told in the native stories, revival follows the havoc brought by the Great Water Serpent. This year his noisy arrival initiated the needed seasonal rains. Indeed, he brought the clouds depicted on his tail in the petroglyphs. A couple of gentle small floods followed, keeping alive the first pools in which tadpoles grew, sustaining the populations of the little spade-foot toads. Some of the trees we thought to be dead leafed-out. Immediately in the arroyo the bare exposed roots sprouted leaves, hiding their pleasing patterns, and the arroyo banks were soon covered in brilliant greenery. Among this finery were the big-leafed elegant and delicate devil's claw and the rare Datura quercifolia, plants that grow only following a major inundation. Above the arroyo, giant sunflowers with big sunny faces graced the line of plant detritus that marked the high-water line, while the banks themselves were awash with yellow as the native gold weed bloomed. From a garden somewhere, seeds of green beans, cabbage, and melons were " planted" as well, although too late for them to mature.

Perhaps sometime during the next hundred years, in another rare appearance, the Great Water Serpent will carry off the heavy truck tire and car frame that he left this time, half buried in the sand in this deceptively familiar arroyo-turned-serpent's-road. The petroglyphs confirm the fact that this guy has been around these parts for a long time. He'll be back.

BLESSING BY THE SPIRIT DEER
by
MAVIS GREER

On a warm July day in 1997 John and I are on our way to visit the Ryegate Petroglyph site. We had known about the site, which overlooks the Musselshell River valley and a small, east-central Montana town, for many years but had never been there. By this time we were three years into a self-driven rock art recording project in Montana, and it was taking us across the state. We were working on getting more information into the State files on old recorded sites that had only minimal mentions, and the Ryegate site was high on our list as it has experienced considerable vandalism from local high school kids who have painted large letters and rude remarks about neighboring town teams that can be seen from the highway.

As we are driving toward town from the west on a two-lane highway that parallels the Musselshell River through the rock-lined valley, it is a day like most others during the summer. The hot sun is bright, striking a contrast between the sandstone cliffs north of the highway where the temperature is probably close to 100 degrees and the green cottonwood trees along the river, which provide a cool place for animals from the mid-day heat. We are riding along in our air-conditioned pickup when we see a large mule deer has been hit in the west-bound lane. Just barely off the east-bound lane (there are no shoulders on the road) is a car with Alaska license plates. A young couple is standing by the car, with the young man trying to call for help on his cell phone, but since there is little to no cell service in the area he wasn't having any luck. The deer was not dead, but it was hurt too badly to stand up and get off the highway. However, that was not preventing it from trying to stand, which was really heartbreaking to watch.

Quickly assessing the situation we knew that if a vehicle came down the highway traveling west there could be a bad accident since it would either hit the deer, which was partially sitting up, or the two people standing by the Alaskan car. So, we pull off the road, and John gets out with the gun we have in the truck. Not taking time to talk with the young couple, who aren't paying any attention to us anyway, he dashes to the deer in the road and is able to grab ahold of its head and pull it off the road into the grassy ditch. Once the deer is in the ditch, John shoots the crippled deer putting it out of its misery and sending it over the rainbow bridge. While all of this is going on, I stay by our truck and the young couple is doing nothing, not even appearing to notice what is happening with the deer. They don't approach us or yell to us from their vehicle. After making sure the deer is dead, John returns to the truck, and we continue on our way without speaking to the two kids who are still trying to get their cell phone to work. As we drive off, we can see them still standing by their car along the road, and we wonder if they are thinking "who was that gun-toting man?"

The Ryegate Petroglyphs are located near the top of a high sandstone bluff north of the Musselshell River valley. Because the site is separated from town by a steep slope with tiers of sandstone cliffs in order to get to the site by vehicle you have to drive north of town and circle back through an area of gentle slopes with open grasslands and ponderosa pine groves. The pine parkland along this approach is a beautiful landscape and provides easy driving to the site. On foot, it is possible to access the site climbing up the steep slope, especially if you're an agile young high school student looking for something to do in this small town. However, regardless of how one gets there, the site has had extensive visitation since the original petroglyphs were placed there by local Indian tribes, who made the images prior to the coming of the horse to this area in the early 1700s. Beginning in the 1880s names, initials, and dates were inscribed into the wall, but by the mid 1900s high school kids started painting the site, first with brushes dipped in paint cans and later with the readily accessible spray paint. However, the pre-contact petroglyphs continue to sustain their esteemed position on the wall, and even with all the overwriting, they are not letting their messages be wiped out by these later people coming into the area and using the site to display theirs.

About a half hour after the deer incident we are driving along the dim two-track on the backside of the sandstone cliff toward the rock art. Just before arriving at the petroglyphs a pure white mule deer comes out of the trees and crosses the meadow in front of us. Albino deer and antelope are extremely rare, and we had seen only a couple of albino animals before, but never a full-grown mule deer. We are in awe as it walks in front of us and stop the truck to watch it. The message the deer is sending as it pauses to look at us is "thank you for sending me to the spirit world." Neither of us doubted the message, and the fact that it waits to appear to us until we are almost at the site reinforces to us the tie of the rock art to the spirit world and its ability to influence life in this world. That day we feel unquestionably blessed by the power of the spirit deer.

OFF THE WALL

by

Polly Schaafsma

We're finally finished packing the mules and leave the rim, heading down a rocky trail toward the Esplanade. We're a small group—Curt and myself, Tom McCarthy the videographer, Bruce Aikens, his daughter Mercy from Roaring Springs, and Gordon Smith and Jerry Jerman with the mules. I've just had an argument with these cowboys about Cynthia's big canteen of water that she left for us on her parked car at the top. Per her request, I had promised to bring it down, but these guys refused to add it to the load, insisting that we'd have all the water we'd need without it. Gordon and Jerry are not only packing in our gear for a several days' camp, but they are also going to keep us supplied with water from the nearest spring about a mile and a half from the painted rock shelter that is our destination. No need to burden the mules with Cynthia's canteen.

Cynthia and Renee, a park ranger, are down at the site already, saying that they wanted to enjoy it alone for a couple of days before our 'mob' showed up. I have been contracted by the National Park Service to record these recently discovered rock paintings in a non-descript overhang along a little stony terrace in the Esplanade, the broad, dissected, arid shelf inside Grand Canyon above the dark slit of the inner gorge. By this time in 1987 several of these painted sites had been found in the area and Shaman's Gallery, our goal, was noteworthy among them.

The descent into Tuckup is pretty easy, compared with the steep drops into the canyon further east. But the space this drainage encompasses feels infinite. One could spend a lifetime right here and never get to really know the place. It is early September and hot. The muleteers point out a bright green spot at some distance to our left, the location of the spring, our water source, but we continue our descent, eventually reaching a large flat along which runs the sandstone ledge and the overhang harboring the paintings. Soaring over the ledge is the painted surface that has inspired this expedition. From up there, Cynthia and Renee holler down their greetings, and ask immediately about the canteen that by this time is almost 5 miles away. I explain, but they are disgruntled. In spite of their cantankerous mood, we join them on the ledge and inspect the panorama of fantastic anthropomorphic entities all packed tightly together and on top of one another, painted in unprecedented detail. By now I have a headache from the heat of the day, and after a brief inspection of the site, and barely comprehending the enormity of my assignment due to the complexity of the painting I am supposed to record, I find a shady nook under the rocks and take a nap.

The recording takes several days during which we adapt to the heat. More Park Service personnel arrive. And leave. Cynthia and Renee depart. Gordon and Jerry and their string of mules appear to be the size of ants against the cliffs in the distance as they go to the spring for our water. When they return, they tell us that there is a dead cow in the front of the spring but that the water in the back is fine. I guess it is. At least the water tastes okay, and no one gets sick.

Perhaps they are "pulling our leg?" We'll never know.

Meanwhile, making the drawings is time consuming and demanding. Everything is photographed with slide film, 1987 being prior to the digital age. Then we literally map the paintings, setting up a grid with Curt measuring with a transit. On gridded paper I mark all the measurements and pencil in the forms and details. Later, all of this will be transferred to acetate as an ink drawing according to the specifications of the National Park Service. I get to explore every detail of this collection of bizarre entities crammed tightly together on the sandstone wall-ceiling. Throughout, carefully painted in white, bighorn sheep are pictured, their realistic forms a sharp contrast with the unearthly spirits that dominate this rock face. Each one of these 'anthropoids' is different—some seemingly half-human and half-plant, or something else entirely. Regardless most are exaggeratedly elongated. One figure with tiny, tiny arms and hands has the crenulated contours of a tomato worm, at once incomprehensible and terrifying. Painted in white, red, and green, some seem to wear rich textiles marked with intricate designs defined in fine thin lines. Their heads are bulbous or lacking altogether, and their elongated non-human body contours often terminate in distinctly human legs and feet and penises that extend down to foot-level. At one end in a heavily painted area, human arms seem to flail in desperation smothered by several other figures painted on top. Few have faces, although one painted in white has large round eyes encircled with long black lashes, the epitome of a Halloween ghost. Casper, for sure.

In the midst of this strange company, one small figure, distinctly human, seems to step slightly away from the others, one hand extended and touching one of these spirit beings, while the other hand waves at me in a friendly gesture. I begin to like this little 'person', and as I draw, we begin to establish a kind of rapport that is somehow reassuring in the midst of a growing feeling of uncertainty generated by these incomprehensible, weird, and perhaps even threatening beings. The little waving guy becomes my friend.

At the end of four days, we pack up and hike out.

Once at home I write my report and begin to trace the penciled images on paper to create an ink-on-acetate version. This takes a great deal of focus and I become immersed in the task. During this time in the middle of the night, I open my eyes, and fully awake, I see all of these figures lined up staring at me at the foot of the bed. This spectacle lasts for one second, perhaps two. At which point they know I see them, and they flee in concert out the bedroom door, their lower bodies swept up like sheets in the wind. Shaken by this incredulous scene, as I stare at the now empty doorway, my friend returns for a moment, and peeking around the edge of the door frame he waves. Then he vanishes with the others. I guess everything is okay.

Petroglyph of the horned serpent moving horizontally across the cliff face toward a face or mask. Above are two large shields. Galisteo Basin, New Mexico. (Photograph by Polly Schaafsma)

Over its banks, the flooded waters of the arroyo make a moving shiny serpentine pattern across the landscape on the edge of the Galisteo Basin south of Santa Fe, New Mexico. (Photograph by Curt Schaafsma)

The morning after the flood. Note the debris. (Photograph by Curt Schaafsma)

Rock painting of the horned serpent with stepped cloud patterns in its body, Rio Grande valley, southeast of El Paso, Texas. (Photograph by Curt Schaafsma)

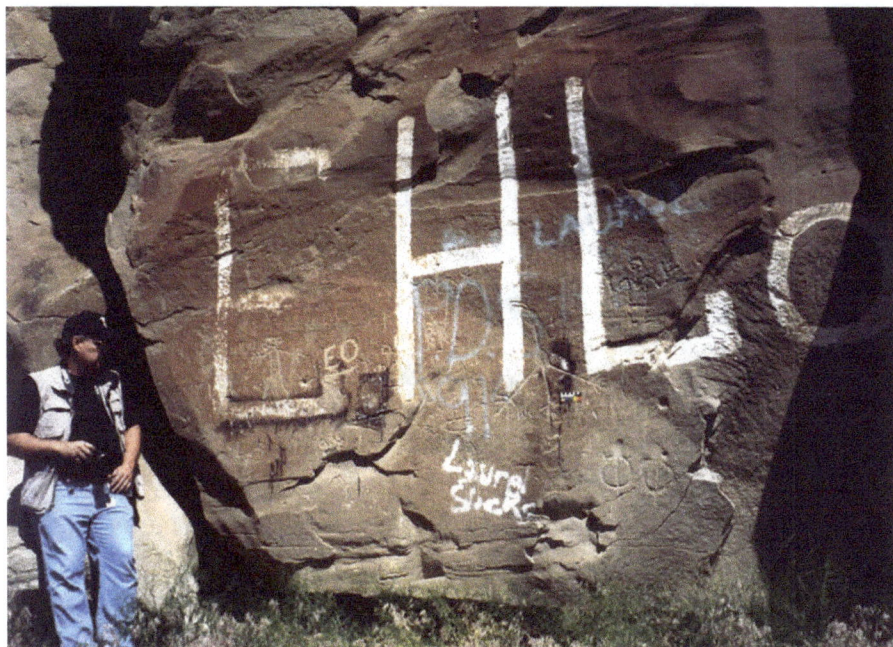

John by the Ryegate Petroglyph (24GV406) main panel.
(Photograph by Mavis Greer)

Typical scenery along the Musselshell River valley in east-central Montana.
(Photograph by Mavis Greer)

View of Ryegate Petroglyph panels relative to the Musselshell River valley below. (Photograph by John Greer)

Spirit deer near the Ryegate Petroglyph site. (Photograph by Mavis Greer)

View of Tuckup, Western Grand Canyon. (Photograph by Polly Schaafsma)

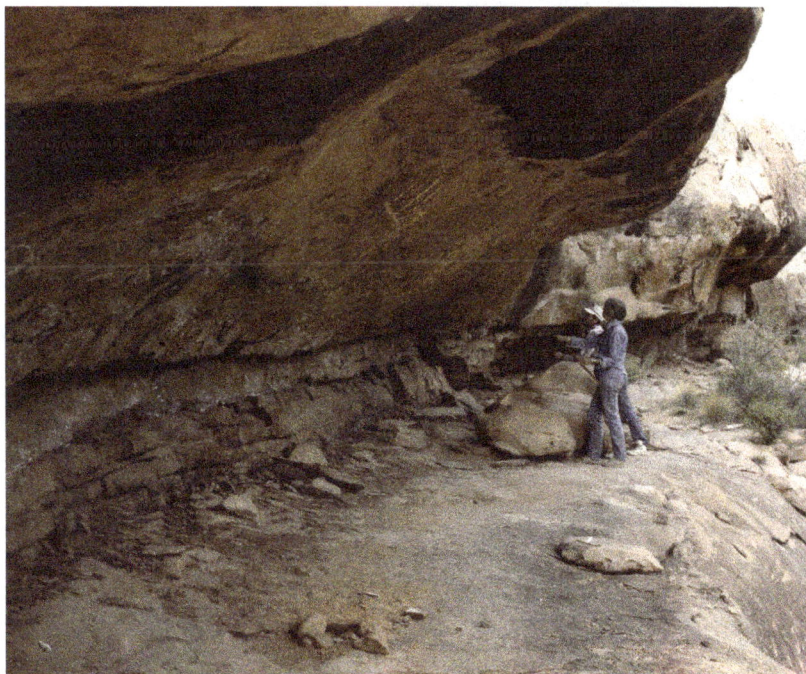

The rock shelter with paintings on the sloping roof.
(Photograph by Curt Schaafsma)

Detail of the painting. (Photograph by Polly Schaafsma)

Mules and cowboys headed to spring for water.
(Photograph by Curt Schaafsma)

Painting on the left side of the panel. (Photograph by Polly Schaafsma)

Polly recording the paintings. (Photograph by Curt Schaafsma)

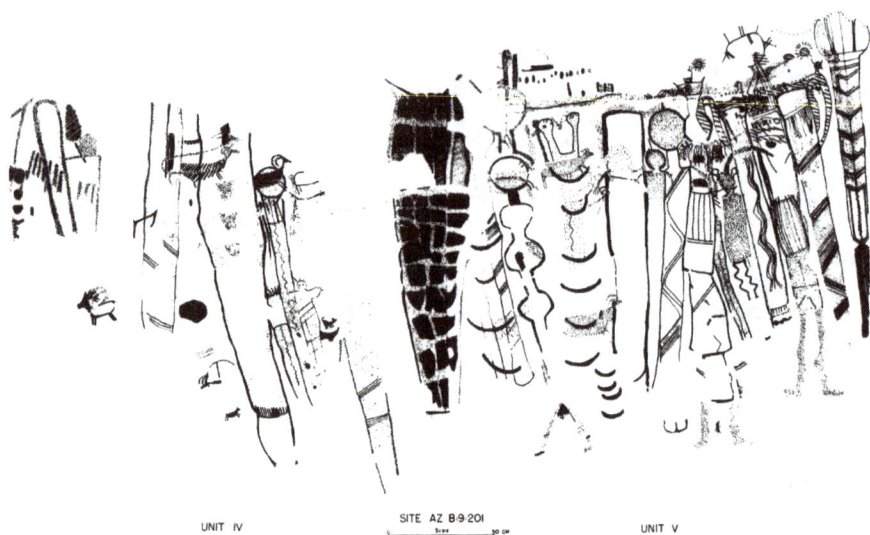

UNIT IV   SITE AZ B·9·201   UNIT V

Polly's drawing of the central figures.

Drawing of figures on the left showing Polly's little "friend," second from right.

UNIT III

SITE AZ B·9·201

0   Scale   50 CM

4
PEOPLE WE MEET ALONG THE WAY

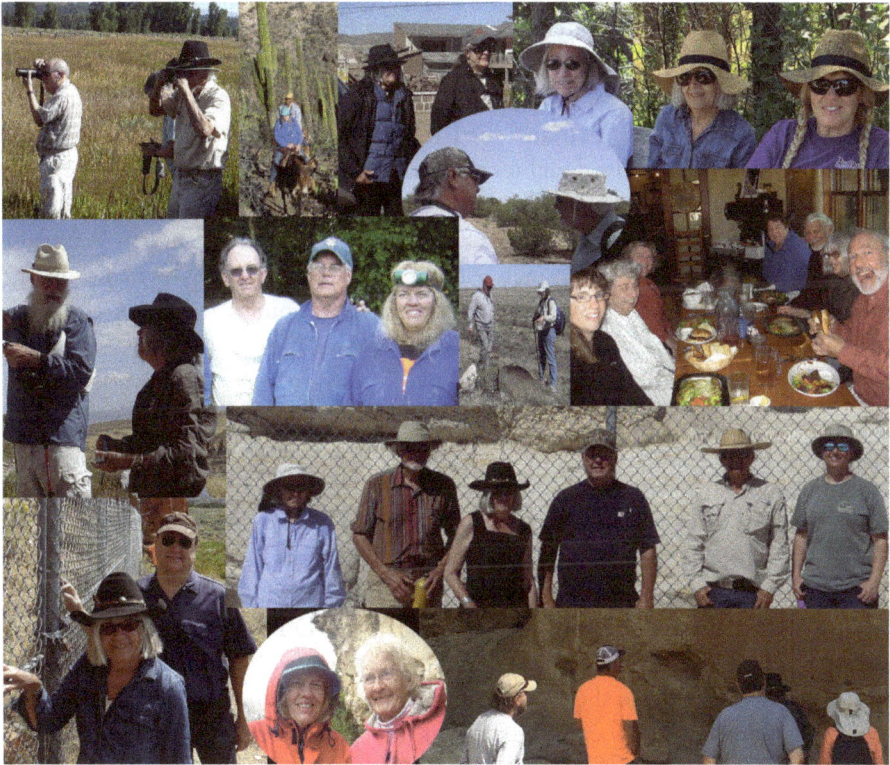

Composite of friends during site visits. (Photos by John and Mavis Greer)

ROCK ART AND THE SECRET SERVICE
by
Mavis Greer

I expect it isn't too often that the Secret Service must visit rock art sites while on duty. However, that was part of their job in 1999. On a hot July weekend John and I were in the backcountry of rural central Montana to visit rock art sites with several people that included the great-grandson of President Teddy Roosevelt, his wife, and the daughter of the then President, Chelsea Clinton. They wanted to visit the Bear Gulch Pictographs, owned by our friend Macie Ahlgren and her family, and Macie had also arranged for us to visit the nearby Atherton Pictographs on her neighbor's ranch. At that time the Roosevelt's owned property in the area, and Chelsea was working with several young people on the large N-Bar Ranch south of Bear Gulch in the Big Snowy Mountains. The N-Bar was an environmentally oriented ranch with an eye toward improving conditions on the ranch through natural and not chemical means. So, they were experimenting with using different good bugs to do in the bad ones instead of using pesticides, and other similar practices.

So, how did we come to be in this situation? The previous December Connie Roosevelt, wife of Teddy 4, contacted me about rock art in Montana. After some snail and emails, we made plans to get together the following July to look at sites in central Montana since that was close to their ranch. During our correspondence, she mentioned that three other couples—the Stocktons, Winthrops, and Elliotts (the latter were owners of the N-Bar at the time)—also wanted to look at the sites. We made plans to meet the night before at the N-Bar and spend the night in the Roosevelt guesthouse. We arrived earlier in the day and spent some time with Macie before the evening found us in one of the barns at the N-Bar listening to a cowboy singer/comic. I think there was some "bug conference" going on there at the time, which was the reason for the entertainment. At that event Connie approached us to see if a few more people could join us the next day, and those people included Chelsea, a friend of hers from France, and the Secret Service. The more the merrier as far as we were concerned.

The Roosevelt guesthouse was in the foothills of the Big Snowy Mountains, and after sleeping well in the mountain air and having breakfast in their well-stocked kitchen, we stopped by the N-Bar to pick up the others going on the tour, including the two Secret Service men, who were in their own vehicle. We then continued north onto the dissected canyon lands where we met Macie.

The sunny and hot July day begins at Atherton Canyon. By the time we are driving along the two-track road leading to the site there are several vehicles in a long line. Since it's not possible to drive into the sandstone-lined canyon, we park the assortment of cars and trucks on the two-track road on the ridgecrest. The normal commotion of getting everyone ready to hike down the steep slopes into the canyon then commenced. Does everyone have a hat? How about water? Bug spray? Sun screen? Finally, we set off across the upper grass-covered ridgecrest to a drainage area where erosion of the sandstone cliff has formed a natural stair-step area where we can drop into where the rock art is located along the base of the cliffs that line the creek. As we spread out walking down into the canyon, we are followed by the Secret Service agents who are slightly lagging behind and stuck out like sore thumbs. Their new clothes, although appropriate for backcountry hiking, were so clean and crisp that they looked like they had just stepped out of an REI advertisement; no one would mistake them for an integrated part of our group, which was more casually dressed and walked along chatting and picking the ripe berries on the numerous bushes to eat as we ambled along. They both carried weapons under their tan-colored vests, which normally would not stand out in the Montana backcountry, although in 1999 there was not the open carry displays that you see twenty years later. They keep their distance during our walk down the canyon. They don't talk with any of us, don't eat any of the berries, and don't show any interest in the rock art. They take their jobs seriously, although we joke that we aren't sure who would be out there that would pose a threat since it was doubtful that there were any other people within miles.

Atherton Canyon is filled with brush in the area of the rock art, so it is necessary to thrash through the dense vegetation to get from one rock art panel to the next. This site contains both pictographs and petroglyphs, and is best known for a style known as Vertical Series. The remoteness of the site, the lack of public access, the protection of the numerous layered overhanging sandstone ledges that comprise the cliff face from natural deterioration caused by water and snow, and dense brush have helped preserve these paintings for hundreds of years. While in the canyon we are carrying on an in-depth discussion about how pictographs and petroglyphs were dated. This is a hot topic at this time as new methods are being developed that can provide more precise ages for rock art never before possible. Cation ratio dating, which is a technique for dating rock varnish that develops over petroglyphs and works by determining the ratio of calcium and potassium to titanium concentrations within the rock varnish, is just coming into use to establish a relative date for petroglyphs. As we are walking out of the canyon Chelsea is explaining the process to one of the women in the group. I am surprised at her knowledge of the process since it's not something people generally know about even peripherally unless they are into rock art or other studies that use the method. Her detailed explanation goes over the head of her listener, and the woman comes over to walk by me and asks if I can just tell her what it is in simple terms.

Leaving Atherton we go to a nearby ranch for lunch. There is a large spread ready in the kitchen for us to dish up buffet style. As we are getting our food, the ranch wife remembers the Secret Service men sitting in their car at the end of the driveway and fills two plates to overflowing for them. We see her walking down the driveway with the filled plates, and just as soon we see her coming back to the house with the plates. It turns out Secret Service people cannot accept food from ranchers, or anyone else, for fear that someone may be trying to poison them. John, who is at the end of the food line, is happy with that policy since he gets their plates.

We leisurely eat lunch spread out through the kitchen, living room, and outside. Some people take time to look at the artifacts collected by the family before we are ready to drive about five miles to the Bear Gulch site. As we're getting organized to go, the son of the ranch family hosting the lunch, who is about Chelsea's and her friend's age, asked the girls if they want to ride to the next site with him. Quickly we see the two girls jump in his pickup, and the three of them speed down the driveway and out onto the county road as they head to the site. Just as quickly we see the Secret Service car speed out of the driveway and onto the county road behind them. I'd be willing to bet that they never expected their job would involve speeding down a dirt road in central Montana toward a rock art site chasing three teenagers in an old ranch pickup.

Since part of our group was already on their way to the site, the rest of us quickly get in our trucks and head that way. Getting to the site we reconvene with the teens and head out for a tour without incident.

Today the Bear Gulch site is open to the public by arranged tours, which can be booked online. It has the largest assemblage of shield-bearing warriors at any rock art site known in North America.

UTAH ODYSSEY: GOLDEN TABLETS, BLOOD ON THE BOULDERS, AND MEETING DEAN BRIMHALL

by

POLLY SCHAAFSMA

It is the summer of 1970 and the manuscript *The Rock Art of Utah* is off my desk and in press. Written in honor of the late Donald Scott, former director of the Peabody Museum of Archaeology and Ethnology at Harvard, the prescribed study was an exercise in analyzing photographs of rock art that Scott had collected. Shortly following his death in 1967, his widow, Louise, was anxious that this special collection of her husband's not be forgotten. Through the years and ahead of his time, Scott had pulled together photographs of rock art from many parts of the world. Knowing of his interest, people from all over the United States and beyond had sent him pictures. Diligently arranged in drawers in a tall, dark green, metal filing cabinet, this collection was known simply as 'The Scott Files'. In the fall of 1968 I traveled to Cambridge to evaluate the files, then housed in a dark, narrow upstairs room in the Peabody Museum. Altogether, the photographs represented a vast area, but only the Utah group consisted of a comprehensive body of data that could be pulled together meaningfully into a book. The terms of my involvement did not provide money to visit the sites themselves. Furthermore, it was Donald Scott's photographic collection *as such* that was of interest to Louise.

The requested files were then sent to the University of New Mexico for my use. Immediately, upon my completion of the project, Jess Jennings at the University of Utah, who shared some of the Utah data with Harvard, offered me a small grant to actually visit some of the sites. He wanted me to gather more inclusive information about them, such as the real extent of the rock art at a given location, that the photos did not necessarily cover. A broader understanding and documentation was needed about their setting. Data on any associated archaeological material were also missing. This was a superb opportunity to finally see the rock paintings and petroglyphs I had written about—a backwards approach to be sure, but such were the circumstances of the case.

The Scott Files photographs were highly variable in quality and in the amount of information that accompanied each photo. Almost everything was in black and white. A number of them were taken by expeditions to Utah that emanated from the Peabody Museum itself, such as the Claflin-Emerson Expedition in 1931. (See *The Crimson Cowboys* by Jerry D. Spangler and James M. Aton, University of Utah Press, 2018.) Some were contributed by locals. Many were stapled to 5x7 filing cards bearing additional written commentary, some of which was curious. Interpretations of abstract petroglyphs, common in Western Utah, were thought to be related in meaning (and form) to Egyptian hieroglyphs. The Ankh was a popular interpretation of one element among a myriad of typically irregular Archaic designs. Knowing just a little about Mormonism at that point, I figured that such observations were the projections of local residents. A few more recent photographs had been submitted by a Dr. Dean Brimhall. These, being colorful and accompanied by insightful comments by Brimhall himself, naturally caught my attention. Not only were the photos themselves of superior quality, but so were their subjects—mysterious but distinctive complex anthropomorphs, that collectively I named the Barrier Canyon Style, based on the "type site"—the Great Gallery located along Barrier Creek. The notes in the files from the 1930s also referred to the drainage as Barrier Canyon.

Guided by information in the files, we write letters ahead, making inquiries as to site locations on public lands managed by the US Forest Service and the Bureau of Land Management. Once in Utah, we talk with ranchers, many of whom are enthusiastic about telling us about Butch Cassidy and his friends. We eat it up! (We have just seen the movie with Robert Redford and Paul Newman.) I also have to explain to ranchers about why I had inquired about Barrier Canyon, when on todays' maps this drainage is called Horseshoe Canyon. In the old files, they referred to it as 'Barrier,' because Barrier Creek runs through it, but the cowboys and locals prefer Horseshoe. It's more 'cowboy'. The issue may be a topographic one, if Horseshoe refers to a horseshoe bend in the canyon, while 'barrier' is reference to the fact that the canyon is difficult to cross. I confess that I settled on 'Barrier' because I thought that "Horseshoe Canyon style" sounded clumsy.

On the first leg of our expedition, however, we begin our field survey with the more enigmatic, less figurative petroglyphs. Near Fillmore on the western flanks of the Wasatch there is a boulder covered with typical abstract, curvilinear-style petroglyphs that I want to check out. This style of petroglyph occurs widely throughout the Great Basin from the Wasatch, across Nevada, to eastern California, and it was defined and named by Robert Heizer and Baumhoff nearly a decade earlier. The Forest Service told us in advance that the site is very well known, and that if we stop by their office, someone will be available to take us there. On arrival we are met with a courteous employee, whom we'll call Paddy, who tells us to meet her at two o'clock on the road east of town heading into the mountains. This will not take us to the rock I have in mind, however, as that would be in the desert basin in another direction. So, off to something new—although I am skeptical. Most of the regional rock art is not in the mountains.

We meet as planned, and Paddy has brought along a friend. We follow them, driving some distance up the mountain canyon until we finally stop below a large cliff face. "They're up there," they point, while Paddy's friend hands us some mimeographed papers with information about the rock art—stipulating that they should be returned. The text and drawings on the papers are by José, they tell us, a guy from Mexico who had provided a 'translation'. They leave, and somehow, I figure I'll leave the prescribed reading for later, after I've seen the rock art and gathered my own impressions. By now, I'm suspicious that they might be "Egyptian" or something like that.

Access is easy enough. A newly bulldozed track leads right up the hill to the cliff where the petroglyphs are supposedly located, and as we begin the climb we notice a recently posted renewed gold mining claim on a tree at the foot of the slope. Reaching a level spot in front of a cliff, it is apparent that a person from a local town has recently posted his claim for another year of legal digging. He has been busy. Machinery surrounds one or two very deep pits, and the place is a little like a small industrial park.

The petroglyphs are on a cliff face around a corner. There, neatly inscribed in several even lines with a metal tool, is a series of miscellaneous individual icons all in the same scale—a skull, human hands, a head in profile, a pitched-roofed house, chevrons, a leg, a set of parallel lines and a bunch of other odd symbols. They have a pseudo-Egyptian look, a little like something that might be conjured up in a Boy Scout notebook. The United States Forest Service has sent us *here*? What in the world were they thinking? At this point, we get out the papers we have been handed—certainly we need to be enlightened. And we are. The mimeographed words inform us that these glyphs were written by the finger of the Angel Moroni to inform whomever should be so fortunate as to find these writings in the brushy wilderness, that here lie the second set of Golden Tablets, buried in ancient times. Furthermore, there are detailed instructions on how to find them. Directions are specific—in cubits—on how far to dig down and then sideways and so forth and in what direction in order to encounter more holy words of guidance from the Angle Moroni. And, by golly, this local enthusiast is on to it.

When we return the papers to Paddy, she naturally enquires enthusiastically about what we thought about the site. We politely tell her that we are looking for more ancient rock art of an indigenous nature and that we think the engravings are recent, where upon she becomes indignant. "They've been there a long time," she says, "for as long as I've been around, and I've been here for thiry years!"

Late that night, camped in forest in the slopes above Beaver, we speculate around the campfire. What is going on with this inscription? Is it a plot to take over the Mormon church? Is José going to show up from Mexico with pseudo-golden tablets and plant them in the hole for Mr. Digger to find? Are they in cahoots? A second set of tablets could certainly stir things up, depending on what was inscribed on them, and with José as a translator, hence therefore acquiring status in the church, he could benefit handsomely from the tithes. We go on to imagine how as "rock art experts" what our own role might be in this nefarious scheme. We plot. Our imaginations run wild. Suddenly I feel paranoid, and the dark woods beyond the light of our fire seems to be teeming with Mormon spies. Okay, shut up, I say—this nonsense has gone far enough.

We always did wonder about José.

The next day we move on to Richfield where we again contact the United States Forest Service office and they direct us to a woman whom we'll call Mrs. Allen. She is their local expert in petroglyphs. With her phone number in hand, Curt makes the call. She answers. She is enthusiastic beyond bounds at the opportunity to share her knowledge. They have a long conversation. Not only does she invite us immediately to dinner at her house, but she assures Curt that at one of the rock art sites she has in mind that she will show us "the most ancient and evil of all symbols." Curious, Curt asks what it is, "The phallus!" she responds.

This is going to be interesting.

Dinner is delicious—a solid, home-cooked meal of meat and potatoes and New England style apple pie. While waiting for the table to be set, I notice a family genealogy displayed along with scattered papers on a table in the middle of the living room. Glancing at it, I see that both Mr. and Mrs. Allen hail from Connecticut. With New England ties myself, I am impelled to read further, but in short order I run into references to Abraham, and not long after that, Adam and Eve. Okay. With this bit of orientation, it dawns on us that we are indeed within a 'foreign country' with the outward guise of middle America. But we are getting used to it. Aren't we?

After the sumptuous meal for which we are duly grateful, Mrs. Allen sweeps us off to the first of "her" sites—one of several she has lined up to show us. One is the location of the ancient symbol she had mentioned on the phone, and she is especially eager to show it to us. At least this time, we are driving in the right general direction, and it isn't too long before we leave our cars and climb a boulder-covered slope. Here, the rocks are carved with Great Basin Curvilinear style petroglyphs (e.g., Heizer and Baumhoff, 1962). It is among these that "the most ancient and evil" resides, and Mrs. Allen loses no time pointing it out. There it is amongst all the other pecked lines and squiggles—it looks like a case of pareidolia to us, but we certainly do not challenge her interpretation. She goes on to explain that these petroglyphs were not created by local Indians, but by a superior race that had lived here prior to their time. And now our well-meaning guide wants to show us another petroglyph site where complex rituals had been conducted by these wise and wondrous early inhabitants of Utah.

Now—groaning a little—we follow in our car. This time the site is near a farm, and the vegetation on the petroglyph hill has all been consumed by their sheep and goats. The ground is essentially bare. The top of the rise is quite flat, and at the summit rests a large boulder of significant dimensions. Petroglyphs cover the top and sides. Here, as is frequently the case, among the circles, dots, and miscellaneous ambiguous configurations, long, continuous grooves are pecked that run between the circles and lines and other things and across the top and down the sides of the boulder. Some seemed to lead to or depart from a depression on the top of the rock. Our diligent guide explains that this was a sacrificial altar where animals—presumably sheep and goats—had been slaughtered, and the blood ran down and all around. Mrs. Allen becomes very excited by the whole thing as she imagines it all in active detail. She explains that the biggest depression was where they put the liver, that the kidneys went somewhere else, and the heart—best of all—the heart—had the place on honor in the little swale on top. Having worked herself into a frenzy, she is keen to take us to more sites tomorrow. Citing our limited schedule, we graciously decline and move on.

We will be heading south and east to Canyonlands and the Great Gallery.

It feels good to get back to solid red rock country and away from those damned boulders and Moroni inscriptions. And besides, if Dean Brimhall should be in Fruita, where we understand he currently lives, maybe we can meet this astute person who made such good observations on those colored photos he sent to Donald Scott. It is a nice thought.

In Fruita we stop by the Capitol Reef National Monument office and make inquiry as to Dean Brimhall's whereabouts. The ranger we talk with is not encouraging. She says that he is quite elderly, busy, reclusive, and uninterested in talking with anyone. If we are lucky we'll get 10 minutes with him. She explains further that his interest in the regional rock art had occurred when he was around 70 years old, and from that time on he had made an extensive photographic record of every site he could find. That collection, accompanied by copious notes had recently been stolen from his car, throwing him into a desperate effort to replicate everything. Under these circumstances, talking with strangers amounted to time lost.

We sympathize, but we still want to talk with him. With directions to his residence, we drive away to find him.

In the shady yard of a house, on a street protected from the hot noonday sun by tall trees, we encounter a frail-looking, thin, elderly gentleman assisting a young man fastening a tall aluminum ladder to the roof of a small jeep. Assorted items of camping gear are scattered about on the ground. Another jeep, a Wagoneer, is parked nearby. The young man is focused on his task of tying down the ladder, while the older man, Dean Brimhall himself, walks over to see what we want. We apologize for intruding, but explain who we are and what we are doing, indicating that we are on our way to the Great Gallery. I told him I had been impressed by his photographs in the Donald Scott files and that I had made good use of them while writing up the Utah collection. He could care less. He is cordial enough, but cold, during our 15 minute conversation. (But, hey, we got a whole 15 minutes with him and were pleased. And besides, in a couple of hours he would have been on his way to wherever—he didn't mention where he and the young man, his grandson, were headed).

It is still early in the afternoon, and we decide to make a side trip to the paintings at Temple Mountain Wash in the San Rafael Reef before the long drive out to Barrier, otherwise known as Horseshoe, Canyon. The dirt road east off Utah Highway 24 to Barrier (Horseshoe) Canyon runs for almost 30 miles toward the Green River drainage, following contours and dips in the topography across a sparsely vegetated red clay and sandy landscape. A few imposing buttes provide definition for wide purple and pink vistas bordered by distant mesas that seem to mark the edge of the world. Close by, rusted and dilapidated stock tanks and other cast-offs from former ranch activity sit silently by the wayside, signs of more prosperous ranching days. There are no cars on the road, not even an occasional ranch vehicle. We pass the turn off to Robber's Roost, continuing on, until a small sandy track leads off to the right through stands of rice grass. Five miles later we reach the slickrock at the edge of canyon.

Unsurprisingly, no one else is there. This is 1970 and the rock art in the canyon depths below us is not yet well-known. Furthermore, it is a hot day in July. We park, welcoming the opportunity to stretch our legs after the long slow drive, and contemplate a spot to set up camp. Setting up camp means parking the pickup on level ground, selecting a comfortable sandy place to throw our sleeping bags, and deciding where to build a campfire. And hot as it is, the idea of a 'camp' without a fire is inconceivable. In those days a campfire was not forbidden, and a small fire made from locally scrounged wood is a welcome focus to any evening under the stars.

We aren't there for more than five minutes when we hear the sound of approaching vehicles and over the hill appear the Brimhall jeeps. So this is what they were up to!

Mr. Brimhall is not one bit thrilled at having company out here on the edge of 'his' canyon. We are clearly regarded as uninvited intruders into what he feels is his private territory. Downright stand-offish, he sets up a tent nearby while most of the time, his back is toward us. We prepare and eat our dinner. As Curt, Pieter our small son, and I and our two dogs convene around the fire, we notice that their camp looks pretty bleak. Feeling at least obligated, we invite our unfriendly neighbors to join us, but they turn down our offer. After a while, however, the campfire is so welcoming and with the evening air now cool, it is more difficult to resist—it is much more appealing than their dark digs. It is probably after ten o'clock, when Dean makes tracks to our camp and sits down.

I cannot begin to recall all that was discussed in the ensuing four hours, but we cover just about everything. Like Aborigines meeting in the desert, we establish our identities. We learn that he is a Jack Mormon with a home in Salt Lake City and member of a notable family within the Mormon Church. He tells us that he rejected the Mormon faith long ago, and that he was the first Utahan to drive a car across the United States. This adventure occurred in a 1913 Packard when all the roads were dirt, and cars designs displayed their genetic heritage from buggies. We heard an impassioned rendering of his 'conversion' to the knowledge he had gleaned from the Barrier Canyon Style rock art and how at the age of 70 it had changed his life. These paintings had awakened him to the fact that men (and women, I'll add) as intelligent as himself had made these paintings, and that they had insights to share. Since that moment he had dedicated himself to finding and recording every single painting he could find. And he related the sad tale of how he had left all his photographs and notes on the seat of his car and how they had been stolen. Devastated, and with no back up, he was beginning anew, and at 84 years old, time was running short.

Instead of a ten-minute conversation we had anticipated with him originally, we have to shut him down after hours of talk in the middle of the night. It is about two a.m. when I hesitantly break in and suggest that maybe we should get some sleep. In four more hours the sun will be up, and it is going to be hot and a busy day.

We are up at first light making moves to prepare breakfast in the cool morning air. Busy with camp chores, we notice our big, black dog, Tooki, wandering over to the green tent in which Dean Brimhall is apparently still sleeping. Took, raising his leg takes a long and satisfying dawn pee on the corner. Aghast I *hope* Dr. Brimhall is still asleep. Thankfully the topic never comes up.

After the usual morning camp activities, we are ready to descend into the canyon—Curt, myself, and Pieter on foot, to be followed eventually by Dean and his grandson, whose name we never seemed to have learned. They will be *driving*—That's what the small jeep is for. And besides, it is always wise to have two vehicles in the backcountry, just in case.

Leaving the Brimhalls behind, for now, we depart. The Wagoneer with most of their camping supplies will remain on top. Negotiating the rough rocky track, which is the remains of an old road that makes its way over tawny sandstone ledges down into the canyon, is a questionable challenge for any vehicle as we are soon to learn as we ourselves scramble over and around big drops amidst sandstone boulders. Near the bottom and well-below the upper cliffs, a long sand dune covers the final talus making for an easy final descent to the canyon bottom. That dune, however, might look less friendly when we climb back out under a hot afternoon sun.

It is July 31st. At the bottom we turn up canyon, passing several other painted panels of Barrier Canyon style rock art en route. At Water Canyon we make a short side junket to refill our canteens and move on. Shortly before reaching the highly anticipated Great Gallery itself, we hear the rumble, then the offensive, grinding noise of the jeep's motor loudly echoing off the canyon walls behind us. As they pass they offer us a lift, but we choose to walk around the next big bend before arriving at our destination.

Soon the great shallow overhang appears in view around the corner, and across the long sweep of the protected pale walls of the alcove, dark, life-size human-like ghostly forms loom like silent sentinels that have minded the canyon for thousands of years. It is around noon and the sun is blasting into the shelter with fury, creating a reflector oven. The heat does not seem to have any impact whatsoever on Dean who by the time we arrive is instructing his grandson about on where to place the aluminum ladder against the cliff in the midst of the paintings in order to make a rubbing of some incised figures he had noticed during his last visit here. Believe me, neither making a rubbing nor placing the scratchy ladder against the wall are accepted practices. But this was 1970, and this was outlaw country in all respects.

While they fiddle with the ladder in what must have been 120 degree heat, with an energetic Dean shouting instructions to his grandson, we take in the paintings for the first time, momentarily ignoring the radiant effects of the blazing sun. The 'Holy Ghost' group suddenly snaps into three dimensions as the appendage-less dark forms near the sprayed "ghost figure", rather than being haphazardly placed alongside now completely encircle it. It is if the cliff is reaching out to grab us and trap us into the circle. And about this time we see another painted form looming over us with a skull-like head and seemingly bound torso. Death. I have the feeling that Dean, himself, is about to disappear and that a new figure will mysteriously appear with his spirit trapped inside. Dean—transformed into a new dark entity—a sort of grease spot—on the wall. Dripping with sweat, and perhaps by this time, a little delirious, we suggest to a now grumpy grandson that perhaps we should find some shade somewhere and eat lunch. Later the sun will have passed beyond the lip of the alcove leaving it shaded.

He is immediately receptive to the idea, and in spite of a few weak objections from his grandfather, we all pile into the jeep and drive up the canyon—about two miles according to my notes—where we finally find shade and relief from the sunny glare. There is a spring here as well, and nearby, is a small group of Fremont paintings, and early historic inscriptions. They are too early to be those of the

Wild Bunch—Butch Cassidy's gang who hung out at Robbers Roost in the flats above the canyon at the turn of the last century. The date 1879 is visible in the slide we took. Leonard Hardy, Will (ard?), and Moore are decipherable or so we think. Here or perhaps elsewhere, Dean pointed out the names of Blue John, who was a member of the gang and "Biddlecome." As we recall, it seems that the latter may have been inscribed by Pearl Biddlecome Baker herself, who grew up on the Robbers Roost Ranch.

By the time we return to the Great Gallery, a shadow has moved into the alcove. Following the acquisition of a successful rubbing by the Brimhalls, and photos by us, we head back. The hike is uneventful, and they soon pass us in their jeep as we wave them on. But at the dune we catch up. As we approach we notice that the jeep is stalled in the deep sand with them fussing around it. Submerged up to the axels! They are at a loss as to what to do even though they have been plying the backcountry for some time now. Luckily the jeep had a winch, and luckily Curt was well-versed in getting vehicles out of a predicament like this. After finding a log (a so-called 'dead-man') to bury with winch attached we were able to pull the little jeep out of this sandy trap. Or perhaps, better said, it pulled itself out once it had something to "grab." We all reach the rim of the canyon without further ado.

But as the Brimhalls are packing up, getting ready to leave, they discover that the Wagoneer won't start—it's dead as a rock. They will have to repack, stuffing as much as they can in the smaller jeep, leaving the Wagoneer sitting there for another day. At least. Silently we all recognized their plight had they been alone out there, with the small jeep stuck, waiting for someone to miss them. There were no cell phones then.

THE CHINA CONFERENCE
by
Mavis Greer

One of the many places archaeologists meet people along the way is at conferences. Archaeologists are big on networking at these get-togethers over food and drink, well, mainly drink. However, in July of 2014 networking took on a whole new meaning for a small group of us foreigners spending a week in southwestern China.

I traveled to Guiyang, China, for the International Federation of Rock Art Organizations Congress by myself as John had decided he wanted to stay home and catch up on other things. I was not worried about traveling half way around the world to a country where the only word I could really remember in Chinese was 'hello,' which I phonetically remembered as "knee how." In Beijing, I had a complicated airline switch and had to take a train to get from the international to domestic terminal, but all went smoothly. Upon arrive in Guiyang, I was prepared with a printout of the hotel information from the internet to give to the taxi driver. I quickly had a taxi and gave him the paper. Unfortunately, the paper had no information in Chinese letters, and he could not read the English alphabet. That did not deter him though, and he ran around to other drivers and people at the airport until he felt he knew where I wanted to go, and off we went.

It was a rainy, cloudy day in Guiyang, a city of several million people. The city is set amongst majestic karst escarpments between the high buildings, which gave the town a romantic other-world feel. Arriving at the beautiful high-rise conference hotel, I was so happy to immediately see Yasha Zhang, the only person I knew in China. She, along with a couple of students, came running out to greet me and paid the taxi, which was great since I wasn't sure the driver and I could communicate enough to get the payment completed. As I was checking in, I found that the conference was not going to start the next day but instead was starting the day after. This was quite unexpected, and I really had nothing to do as I waited. Luckily, shortly after checking in I saw the only two other people from the US there. Carol Patterson and her significant other, Joe, were in the lobby and said that Daniel Arsenault from Montreal had rented a car and driver and was planning to visit a large cave tomorrow along with Aurora Skala from British Columbia. They invited me to go along, and I was really happy to have the company and something to do.

The next morning we set off in the rain, and had a great time visiting the area of Xuantang, which translates (as I understand it) as earthly paradise and fairyland in the world. We spent our time at the large natural cave, Guanyin, with a fantastic waterfall, 32 cultural Buddhas, and paintings of various Chinese spiritual figures.

After that great introduction to the area, we were ready for the conference to begin the next morning. As we gathered for the Opening Ceremony, a woman came up to ask me if I could announce the first speakers. I was quite surprised, but agreed to do so thinking they had non-Chinese presenters and subjects, which is why I was chosen. However, when she brought me the list, that was not so. I looked at the list and then looked around for help with the names. The woman sitting next to me was from Germany, and she had some knowledge of Chinese, so she helped me with the names, which I dutifully wrote down phonetically on the paper.

The Opening Ceremony was just as you would suppose in China, with much pomp and circumstance. Several dignitaries spoke, and others sat on the stage and were introduced. Everything looked to be going well, but just as the Opening Ceremony ended and the transition was being made to begin the presentations, the monsoon rains resulted in the loss of electricity in Guiyang, sending us all into darkness and the conferenece organizers scrambling to find temporary lighting for the large dark ballroom with no windows to the outside in which we were sitting. Soon an emergency generator brought us some dim lights so that the organizers could decide what to do with the hundreds of people at the conference.

With the loss of electricity the organizers were quick to cancel the presentations for the day, and I was freed from butchering the names and titles of several presenters. They then decided we should all go to lunch with the idea that the electricity may come back on during that time. The conference organizers made sure all of us foreigners (i.e., non-Chinese speaking attendees), of which there were only about 15, were well taken care of, and we were kept in a group at all times and fed together, which was really good as it relieved a lot of stress we might have otherwise had. For lunch we were led through the dark stairwells to the restaurant. After lunch we (the non-Chinese) made our way to our rooms on our own, which due to the lack of electricity meant there were no elevators working since the generator was not powerful enough to operate them. The high-rise hotel provided us with much exercise as our rooms were on the 16th and 17th floors. As evening came and we realized the electricity was not going to return, we had an opportunity to get to know one another and our research in a way that we had not expected. Gathering up all the food and drink items from the small refrigerators in our rooms, we all met in Carol and Joe's room for a party. Once there Carol decided we should go around the room and tell our most memorable rock art experience. Quite a variety of stories ensued, including Jean Clottes telling the behind the scenes story about the discovery of Chauvet Cave.

On day two of the conference, a back-up generator provided lights for two conference rooms and power for one elevator, so the conference resumed. At this point the presentation schedule had to be completely reorganized, so it was by word-of-mouth that we learned about which papers were being presented where and by whom, but somehow it worked. I moderated two sessions with the titles and authors handed to me just minutes before the presenters took the podium, but it went smoothly. However, I am sure it was harder on the translators, who were left to do the best they could. Throughout this time our foreigner group was well looked after by the organizers. They gathered us together for breakfast, lunch, and dinner, which although it kept us segregated from the Chinese gave us a great opportunity to bond with rock art researchers from Canada, Mexico, Australia, India, and Germany.

One night the foreigners were treated to a special dinner at one of two places where electricity was restored within the city. One group went to dinner with the mayor of the city, while the group I was with went to dinner with a man from Tibet who has made it his life's work to protect the architectural history of his country. We were seated in a small room of a fancy hotel. The round table supported a large lazy Susan in the center that was filled with food, and as it spun around in front of us, we were to take what we wanted. I was not impressed as a fish with glazed over eyes kept stopping in front of me. I would start the food moving away from me but before I could start to eat that horrible fish would be back in front of me. Needless to say, much of the evening escapes me due to my fixation on the eyes of the fish.

On our last night at the conference, we went to dinner close to the conference hotel in a local restaurant. The restaurant workers were very excited to have so many foreigners eating there, and we had excellent service. They had explained to us that there is no tipping in China, but the woman from Germany felt we absolutely had to tip our waiters since they had looked after us above and beyond the call of duty. After some discussion, she finally realized there was no way that was going to happen. However, the waiters did want one thing in return, a photo of our group with them. It was a great way to end a conference that resulted in such a great bonding experience.

WHAT'S YOUR SIGN? MELANIE AND THE NEW MEXICO ROCK ART SURVEY

by

POLLY SCHAAFSMA

We'll call her Melanie.

Kyle (also a pseudonym), the project photographer, has just asked me if it would be all right if she comes along. I have to say 'yes.' She is his girlfriend after all, and if he wants her on this field expedition it is okay with me. I have to admit, though, I am little skeptical. The fact that she is standing right there in front of me wearing high-heeled sandals she has just purchased for the trip, adds to any previous doubts I might have had.

Kyle, whom at this point, I'd known for over ten years has secured a grant from the New Mexico State Planning Office to photograph rock art in New Mexico. Our idea is to travel throughout the state and document rock paintings and petroglyphs, largely poorly known at the time, and eventually publish a nice book with good photographs. When Curt and I arrive at Kyle's house in Santa Fe with our pick-up truck and our two boys, Pieter and Hoski, aged seven and eleven, Melanie is there ready to go.

Melanie had been around a while. She arrived in New Mexico with Bill, whose photograph had appeared not long before on the cover of *Saturday Evening Post* in which he was all painted up and stoned on LSD, tripping out in Central Park. He described to us how he had looked up to see a camera in his face and then they ran off never even getting his name. Such were the days. The article inside referring to the photo was about the hippie movement sweeping the country in the late 1960s.

I first ran into Bill and Melanie as I was riding my horse along a dirt road in Valdez in the Hondo Valley north of Taos. They had just rented an old adobe building, an abandoned morada once owned by the local Penitentes, and they were standing around outside when I rode up and stopped to chat. Melanie's demeanor was quiet. She was tall and statuesque, and straight, blond hair framed her perfectly oval face and pale countenance in a way that reminded me of women in Flemish paintings. With the appropriate drawl, she said she was from Dev-ai -ne, Texas.

After that initial encounter she was just "around", hanging out with hippies who had "invaded" Arroyo Hondo. And she made the rounds. I barely knew her. After a bit, however, she became widely known as Crazy Melanie, or Eerie Melanie. Either term would do. It was generally recognized that she was strange, a bit off, so to speak.

Then there was that scary incident one cold, early spring night about a year later. Curt was away on an archaeological project, and I was at home with the kids and dogs in our small adobe house in Arroyo Hondo. It was about two a.m. when I suddenly was awakened to the heavy stomping of big feet making several circuits around the building. He (obviously) was going around and around, looking for the door. I was terrified. The dogs barked non-stop. Then he found the damned door and began pounding on it hard. I was glad it was thick. Well, I thought I'll pretend no one is here and just be quiet. But then the boys woke up and began screaming, "Mommy, Mommy..."

Oh, crap! I was stuck—so I answered. "Who is it?" I yelled. I expected to hear back from a drunk neighbor or someone local (or maybe not) who had lost his way. But I was scared to death! A deep voice boomed from the other side. He began a lengthy oration describing how his sports car had lost its brakes at the top of the hill where the road starts to wind steeply down into the valley, and that he had managed to negotiate the whole thing until he reached the tight curve at the bottom, where he lost it, overturning the car. All of this in a thick, but cultured New York accent. He explained endlessly that he was really a good driver but that as good as he was at wheeling around all those curves at an uncontrolled high speed in the descent, that the last curve was too much and he had crashed. Could he please come in and call the police. His car was upside down in a nearby field across the road.

After about 10 minutes of this and disarmed by his New York accent and his obviously shaken condition, I let him in. Probably foolishly—I could have called the cops myself and had him wait outside in the cold. But I let him in, and I was lucky that he was honest. He was okay but a nervous wreck. For two hours this big, rather homely man paced the floor while we waited for cops who never showed up. Traumatized about having destroyed his precious car, he talked non-stop in a loud voice as he paced—and in an endless solitary dialogue he described what a good driver he was in spite of it all, and how he had left New York and come to Taos to be a writer, and was hoping to get started on a new career. (He later opened an art gallery and sold my work.)

Suddenly out of the blue, he mentioned that he had a woman out there in the car. What? There is a woman out there? Left behind in the cold? Is she hurt? What is going on? Why didn't you... For God's sake bring her in! What was he thinking? Or not thinking? Was he ashamed?

Within about 10 minutes he returned with "the woman." In sidled an unruffled, calm, and unhurt Melanie. I have to admit I was startled and relieved. Why hadn't she come with him in the first place. They had been headed to her apartment in lower Hondo when the accident happened. What was he doing with *her*—well...okay. Without hesitation she began a long account of the whole evening and relayed in utter confidence her informed astrological understanding of why this whole thing had transpired. Nothing about the trauma of the crash. More important to her was that she believed it was all due to their prior social engagement with Chuck who lived with his wife in an abandoned yellow, partially underground house up on the mesa—a place widely known as the "Yellow Submarine." Chuck she knew was an innately evil being because of his birth date, she said. They should not have associated with him. She went on quite a while about the birth date, and she knew all about it because she had once been married to a guy born on that same day and he was evil too. By this time I was getting curious about this cursed birth date, so I asked her what date that was. "October twenty-fourth," she answered. I choked on that bit of information and told her that she was in double or triple trouble because that was my birthday too.

I can't recall what happened next, but I think they gave up on waiting for the cops and left—walking the mile and a half down the road to her place. Two days later, the cops arrived.

Several years had passed by the time we drove down from Taos to join Kyle for the two week rock art trip. Once at Kyle's house, we needed to get our act together, assemble all our stuff, and pack for the expedition

Melanie is sitting on a couch doing yoga with Kyle's mother, Margaret. Margaret who is friends with everyone, trying to enlist them in her cause, seemed to like Melanie. Margaret, whom we always thought a little strange as well, was a tall elderly woman with a high squeaky voice, and she was also said to be the head of the communist party in New Mexico. We also understood that that periodically she ran down to the border to join a guerilla group where she learned military skills, we supposed. It was kind of a field camp. I recall that Kyle had her phone number in Mexicali posted on a piece of paper on the wall by his phone in the kitchen.

Somehow or other, my alleged evil astrological associations did not discourage Melanie from wanting to go along on the rock art expedition. Eventually, however, I gained the impression that Kyle had asked me if she could come along because he really didn't want to give her the green light himself and had wished I'd said no. But sullen Kyle, was not the type who would speak his mind, and I agreed, and here we are.

One problem is clear immediately, and that is that no one has any money. We have been promised an advance for the trip by the State Planning office and none has been forthcoming, and, first things being first, we are hungry right now and need to eat dinner, and there is no food anywhere. Kyle's fridge has a pound of hamburger, ketchup, and a bottle of beer, that doesn't even belong to him. The food belongs to Gene and his girlfriend, who at the time are renting a room in Kyle's house, but they are away somewhere at the moment, and having no choice, we eat it all up. On their return, however, Gene and his girlfriend are quite angry.

The next morning Kyle and Curt go down to the appropriate State office and demand some action. Fortunately, the promised and much needed and undelivered check, is sitting on the director's desk. Amen.

It is early July, and heading south, we are experiencing a horrific drought prior to the hoped-for monsoon rains. Underway in our truck, the boys, and gear are in back under the tarp-covered rack, and Curt, myself, Melanie and Kyle are lined up in the cab in that order from left to right in front, a pattern that prevails throughout the trip. The weather is hot and so are we, sweating all crammed together like that. There is no air-conditioning in our 1967 Chevy.

Our first goal is a ranch near Quemado where we understand the ranchers will be glad to show us around. Along the way, we stop by Zuni Salt Lake where Melanie tries to cool off by wading into the water, emerging covered with a layer of salt. All I can recall about that was that it was a problem getting rid of it, since our drinking water supply was not sufficient for bathing. That evening we find a place to camp in some hills. There is a view off to the south, and an abandoned metal chair that is appropriated by Kyle, who carries it off some distance from the dinner-making activities (and Melanie) and sits, staring off into a void.

Our goal the next day is the ranch. We are met by the rancher and his wife and a friend ready to drive us around the back-country mesas where petroglyphs abound. It isn't long after our brief introductions—when I hear Melanie drawl out to one of the women, "What's your sa-aign?" Oh, my God! I should never—I'm not prepared for this. Both women turn and quizzically look at me, wondering what they have gotten themselves into, or perhaps even what she means, and suddenly I am rudely awakened to the fact that this trip is going to be a social challenge, quite beyond that of the hassle of being crowded in the front of the pickup. Already I have noticed that Kyle is ignoring her. As representatives of the State of New Mexico, her very inappropriate fixation on astrological matters is causing me, at least, acute embarrassment. I step in, ignoring Melanie, and begin talking seriously about rock art business in an attempt to over-ride Melanie's question. (But have they noticed her high heels, I wonder to myself.) Fortunately, these fine ranch women seem unruffled and take her in stride. We are off to the sites.

Quemado is marginal ranching country at best, and crippled by drought, the scene is grim—along dusty tracks, we pass windmills and dry water tanks surrounded by dead cattle. The petroglyphs we are out to document are on the rocks capping the low mesas surrounding the valleys, and we spend the day traveling through this desolation to several locations. While Kyle photographs the petroglyphs, Curt scouts the vicinity looking for more, and I make notes and records of the pictures Kyle is taking. Melanie meanwhile is negotiating the rocky cactus-laden slopes with utmost care, complaining on occasion when she miscalculates her step. (Our newly-made rancher friends will have plenty to talk about at their next gathering.) But they are enthusiastic about the rock art, and, by way of introduction, they graciously call ahead to ranchers they know near Reserve, who also have rock art on their property. This is an enormous help in Catron County, a former sanctuary for outlaws, and where today ranchers are proud of the sketchy pasts of their forbearers.

On to the south, we continue our project, with ranchers' help, for which we are most grateful. One night the drought is broken by an enormous downpour that initiates the rainy season, and relieving the heat problem at least for a short while. Melanie now is becoming quite bored, crammed in as she is between me and Kyle. To remedy the monotony of the drive and the stress of the sticky July heat, she begins to give vocal expression to unchained mental perambulations that go on endlessly and make no sense. On one particularly hot day, we are treated to such rambles as we drive steep, dirt roads high into the hills near Cliff to a line-camp, above which is a rock shelter with paintings. By now Melanie has big blisters on her feet and can't make the climb, so we leave her at the camp below where she is able to take a cool dip in the stock tank. At some point while we are busy high up the slope recording red paintings, the line-camp cowboys arrive to find a naked Melanie in their tank. Did she ask them for their "sa-aign," I wonder?

Not long after this we arrive at Gila Cliff Dwelling National Monument where we record small painted sites scattered in overhangs above the brushy banks of the Middle Fork of the Gila. Kyle is becoming more and more reclusive and grumpy. New to me is the fact that Kyle has a terrible temper, and at one point he throws his treasured Hassalblad into the brush. I have no memory of why and I didn't know why then either. (I can only recall that he did it). There is no apparent reason for his increasingly gloomy mood and glowering, dark brow, and none is ever articulated, Curt suggests that it is due to years of pent-up anger at me for turning down his marriage proposal back in 1958. I insist that it is obvious that he is annoyed by Melanie. But at the same time, he is increasingly irritating *me* by his mood. And I am particularly annoyed by his conspicuously wasteful use of camp supplies, including the paper towels. Camp-cabin fever.

At the cliff dwellings, we are accompanied by a uniformed ranger into the ruins, and Melanie, evidently impressed by his authoritative appearance, decides to ask his advice about what to do with her sore toes. Totally unprepared for this kind of question—and she may have already asked about his "sign," he stares at her and her high heels in disbelief from under his hat and mutters something about maybe 'ointment', while the rest of us wish that we could just disappear.

We make camp that night in the valley near some hot springs. Following a leisurely breakfast, the boys wander off a good distance from camp where they are fully engrossed with building little roads with their toy trucks. I am busy preparing to wash the breakfast dishes and have dipped a big basin of scalding hot water from a nearby spring. To get this handy hot water, I had had to push aside two dead parboiled frogs that had unwittingly jumped into it. As I stand over the water, waiting for it to cool enough to put my hands into, right in front me and without any apparent provocation, Kyle begins to have a tantrum. He grabs a role of paper towels and ripping off long, white lengths, he throws them to the ground, glaring at me.

"What is wrong with you?" I demand.

"I just had fight with your kids!" he barks back.

You What? A fight with my kids? You—you a grown man had a fight with... with my little boys who were minding their own business?

I look up to see Pieter and Hoski, hand in hand, headed away from their smashed playground and making off into the Gila Wilderness. I am livid!

Apparently Kyle has stomped out their roads, and when they objected he kicked their whole scene apart with his big feet. I'm consumed with a mamma wolf-like anger. I begin screaming furiously at Kyle, and grabbing the dish of hot water getting ready to hurl the whole basin of the scalding stuff into his scowling face! When at that split-second a huge troop of marching, cheery boy scouts and their leaders emerge along the trail from behind a cliff. They have heard every word of my wrath and are grinning expectantly at what from the other side of the rock must have sounded like a good domestic fight. They are all duded up in their uniforms—silly hats, shorts, shirts with all kinds of colored stripes and emblems signaling their goody credentials, the leaders being the most garishly decorated, and they wave and laugh without missing a beat as they march past. Little do they know that they have done their good deed for the day by appearing just in the nick of time to save Kyle from scalded eyeballs!

We begin laughing too, helplessly.

We continue south to the Mexican border where we finish our survey at Picture Cave in the bootheel of Hidalgo County. At least for the time being, site visiting together is over. Not surprisingly, the remainder of the field work was conducted independently.

As we head north, a sense of surrealism seems to engulf everything. Maybe it's the heat, maybe it's Melanie's weird behavior. We stop in Hatchita to see if we can pick up some snacks for lunch. Outside a store there is an ample patch of shade that we eye as a lunch spot. It is the only shade for 300 square miles, or so it seems. Tired, hot, and dirty, having been on the road for two weeks, I imagine that we were a motley lot. We might have even looked like hippies (archaeologists have been known to)—we certainly are not locals. We walk into a rather bare building. Inside, a few sparsely stocked shelves and a bar feel like relics from an earlier century. The proprietor silently stares at us. A piano, covered with thick dust, attracts Melanie's attention, and she promptly goes over to it. While asking the proprietor about her "sign," (first things first), she flips open the protective lid covering keys that may not have been touched in the last decade and plunks out a few notes. The proprietor continues to glare. Then Melanie, apparently now feeling that she has acquired full membership in our project, asks where we might find "hieroglyphs' around there. The woman maintains her blank look seemingly not registering any of this, although by now she is agitated by our strange entourage, and an atmosphere of unfriendliness, even perhaps hostility, pervades everything. We pay for some cold drinks and Fritos and leave. Thinking better of our plan to enjoy the shade of the building, we climb back in the pickup and drive until we come to a tall yucca growing on the side of the road. Leaning a little to the north, it is tall enough to provide shade for all six of us to line up to sit and eat. As the sun moves, the shade moves, and we shift our positions accordingly. One adapts.

Onward through cuckooville. We drive north in silence through desolate desert hills. Heat waves rising over the pavement add to a surreal landscape. Suddenly we noticed things in the middle of the lonesome highway. We look harder. They look like candy bars. We stop the car and get out to check. They really *are* candy bars! Milky Way candy bars. What is this? At first it seems that maybe bored kids in a back seat had thrown them out while their parents unknowingly drove down the road. Then this seems unlikely—there are so many of them and they continue—hundreds and hundreds of them for miles, maybe four or five miles—Milky Way candy bars evenly scattered one by one down the middle of the road—we are driving the Milky Way. Is this a 'Happening' here in the barren desert of Hidalgo County? And why here? Had Melanie managed to successfully conjure up a group hallucination? I personally doubt it, but, there they were, and we'll never know how they got there, and we'll never forget.

At the end of that day we make our final camp on a creosote flat somewhere near Los Lunas south of Albuquerque. A huge thunderstorm pours down buckets, but we are too tired to go on to Santa Fe that night, so in the midst of a wild downpour, we are all trying to find dry spots to hole up—the kids in the cab, Curt and I in the back, and Kyle and Melanie wrapped in a water-proof tarp on the ground. It isn't long before Kyle kicks her out, and suddenly she appears at the back of the truck amidst the lightning flashes, wet and naked partially covered with a sheet of black plastic. She wants to crowd in with us. There is no room. We decline her company, and she crawls under the tailgate for the rest of the night.

If she resented not being let into the tarp-covered truck bed while the rain poured down and the thunder roared, she can attribute my heartlessness to my evil "sa-aign"—I'm off the hook.

THE STEPFORD ARCHAEOLOGIST
by
MAVIS GREER

For those of you that don't know or have forgotten what the novel and subsequent movie the *Stepford Wives* was all about, let me remind you. Ira Levin published this book in 1972 about a town of submissive housewives that turn out to be robots created by their husbands to always look and act perfect relative to their small town norms. Well, while in Portugal on a field trip to a cave in 2006 John and I encountered one of those wives—there can be no other explanation.

We were attending the International Union of Prehistoric and Protohistoric Sciences (*UISPP*) conference in Lisbon, which that year also included in the international rock art conference for IFRAO. Midway through the conference we were taken on field trips to various sites within driving distance. About twenty of us on our bus were going to a small cave with an entrance within a brush-covered, rocky terrain high above the ocean in western Portugal. The driver let us out for a quarter mile walk to the cave entrance. Most of us were dressed for the field, but even then several young women were wearing shorts that soon resulted in bloody legs as we left the previously flat bladed road and started walking cross-country through short sticker bushes. Even those of us with long jeans were getting hooked by the stickers, causing our clothes to be snagged. However, one woman in our group was dressed in a white blouse with large flowers, a pink skirt, and sandals with tiny raised heels. Although this in itself is an unusual field outfit, she topped it off by carrying a nice, handled purse. She looked like she was ready to head to church rather than a cave.

Arriving at the cave, we found there were two entrances. So we entered single file into a small room where there were a couple of archaeologists waiting to tell us about their findings. We came in through a walking passage that was not only dirty but also muddy, and the mud did not remain just on the bottom of most of our shoes. After listening to the story of the cave excavations, we exited the cave by a different entrance that was no more than a large hole, and some ducking down was needed by taller people. By the time we exited the cave, all of us had added dirt to our clothes and exposed body parts except for the pink-skirted lady. She still looked as clean and blood free as when she left the bus. The only way we figured she could accomplish this was by being a Stepford wife. I was so impressed as I walked behind her the last few hundred feet on a dirt road to re-enter the bus that I could not help but take her photo.

Group of visitors walking into Atherton Canyon, central Montana.
(Photograph by Mavis Greer)

Vertical Series rock art panel in Atherton Canyon (24FR3), central Montana.
(Photograph by John Greer)

Chelsea Clinton, Macie Alhgren, and Mavis at Bear Gulch (24FR2), central Montana.
(Photograph courtesy of Macie Alhgren)

Shield-bearing warrior pictographs at Bear Gulch (24FR2), central Montana.
(Photograph by John Greer)

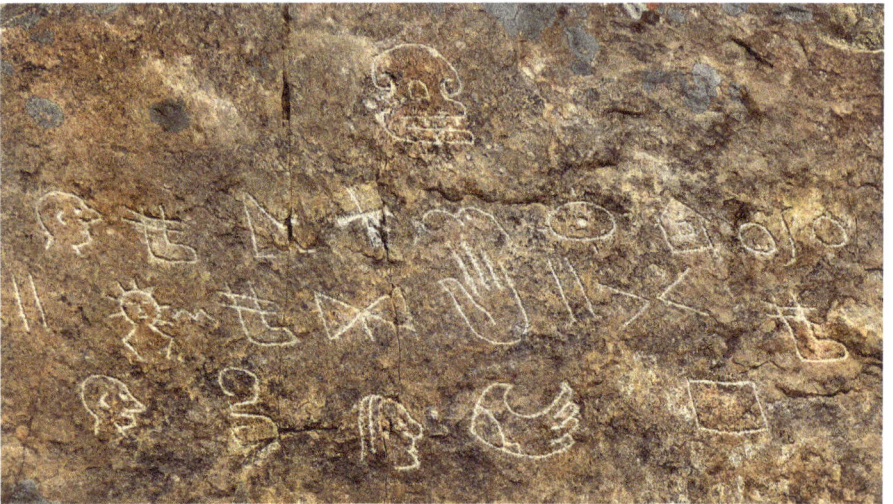

Western Message Petroglyphs near Fillmore, Utah.
(Photograph by Mavis Greer)

Dean Brimhall viewing a Fremont painting in Barrier Canyon.
(Photograph by Polly Schaafsma)

Death figure,' Great Gallery, Barrier
(Horseshoe) Canyon.
(Photograph by Polly Schaafsma)

Three-dimensional composition, Great Gallery.
(Photograph by Polly Schaafsma)

View from hotel room in Guiyang, China. (Photograph by Mavis Greer)

One of the Guanyin cave entrances, China. (Photograph by Mavis Greer)

Walking to a cave in western Portugal. (Photograph by Mavis Greer)

Near a cave entrance in western Portugal. (Photograph by Mavis Greer)

Mrs. Stepford wife on her way back to the bus after visiting a cave in western Portugal. (Photograph by Mavis Greer)

5
HIDDEN STORIES BEHIND SITES

U-Bar Cave entrance in southwestern New Mexico, 1996.
(Photograph by John Greer)

NIGHT CHANT
by
POLLY SCHAAFSMA

In 1963 the gates of Navajo Dam closed, and the waters of Navajo Lake submerged the tawny cliffs of canyon landscapes along the San Juan and Pine Rivers. Vanished were the river banks lined with cottonwoods and pinyon and juniper-filled slopes along with the traces of the people who had once called these places home. For over 2000 years Ancestral Pueblos and then much later the Navajos had built houses, farmed, and inscribed and painted images on the pale sandstone canyon walls. I had just finished my monograph on this rock art for the Laboratory of Anthropology at the Museum of New Mexico in Santa Fe as part of the Navajo Reservoir salvage project.

In contrast with Pueblo petroglyph panels of rather simple broad-shouldered people and animals, brightly colored paintings made by late seventeenth-early eighteenth century Navajos stood out. These in particular had caught the attention of the archaeologists doing the initial surveys, as they clearly depicted the ye'i, or Holy People, featured in contemporary Navajo sandpaintings. I've often thought that they were the reason that the project director, Ed Dittert, had decided to include a rock art investigation in the first place. In 1961 this was a pioneering venture in regular archaeological practice, but paralleled by rock art documentation in concert with the nearby Glen Canyon project to the west, under the supervision of the Museum of Northern Arizona and the University of Utah. There too, the free-flowing waters of the lower San Juan and the Colorado were about to be obstructed by a dam, flooding the canyons and a rich archaeological heritage.

Meanwhile in northwestern New Mexico, El Paso Natural Gas had opened up gas field explorations in the adjacent canyon networks to the south of the San Juan and Navajo Dam, and their roads gave access to places that had previously rested in peaceful isolation in the not so distant past. The Navajo had moved out of the area in the mid-eighteenth century, but during their brief residence there, they made numerous paintings of their religious imagery. As it turned out, the river canyons behind the dam had harbored only the northern margin of this early Navajo rock art.

Rock art did not fail to catch the attention of the gas field workers traveling these sandy, clayey tracks day in and day out, building pipelines, well pads, and continually checking on their facilities. Among these men, Harry Hadlock who had recently immigrated to the Farmington area from Texas, took note. On days off he and his wife, Sally, began exploring and photographing the rock art they encountered, and they quickly became part of the avocational group of archaeologists whose interests in the landscape exceeded that of extracting gas and oil. In his last years, Harry told me that his early enthusiasm for company values had vanished, deeply regretting the damage that was occurring to the land and the archaeological remains and history that it harbored.

We visited often, sharing our common interests and traveling the back country together, as Harry took us to newly discovered sites he had found in the course of his daily work-related travels in the canyons. Delgadito Canyon was special. It seemed that it once must have been a focus for Night Chant ceremonials. A number of panels of paintings featuring the Night Chant Holy People were clustered under rock overhangs in one location. Among these was the most beautifully painted group of all—a panel of elegantly delineated figures in bright colors—Fringemouth, the female god of the Night Chant and others, headed by an exquisitely detailed Ghanaskiddi, the Humpback God. This particular Ghanaskiddi was both incised and painted in azurite blue, turquoise, white, yellow, orange and red. The figure was the most carefully and splendidly rendered Navajo ye'i I've ever seen among the vast number of images made during this period.

One day in the spring of 1965, Harry calls with terrible news. Jess Goodwin, a friend, El Paso employee, rock art aficionado, and fellow member of the local San Juan Archaeological Society, had phoned to report that the rock face bearing the splendid Night Chant paintings has fallen off and is now lying face-down in the rock shelter. Harry suggests that among other things, vibrations caused by the traffic of gas-well trucks rumbling up and down the road below has provoked the dislodging of this precarious rock. Soon after we join Harry on a trip to the canyon to assess the problem. The sandstone slab is huge, and with it fell a line of some of the most exquisitely painted ye'i that have ever been found. The beautiful Ghanaskiddi and a Fringemouth figure, however, remain intact and in place on the cliff to the left.

It isn't long before Bertha Dutton, the newly-appointed director of what was known in those days as the Museum of Navaho Ceremonial Art, gets wind of the rock. The general consensus is that something needs to be done to "salvage" the rock and its paintings, and Bertha is interested in acquiring it for the museum. They would be the only 'original' paintings of the Holy People in the museum's possession. Because sandpaintings themselves are ephemeral and ritually disposed of after a ceremony, the museum had only copies on paper of Navajo ceremonial art. They also had Navajo weavings that were also copies, but the Museum of Navaho Ceremonial art had nothing original. So through the Hadlocks, she begins negotiating with El Paso Natural Gas, who was somehow or somewhat held accountable for this disaster, for the use of one of their huge flat-bed trucks and other equipment to haul the rock to Santa Fe. Once there, it will be installed as an outdoor exhibit on the grounds of the museum.

But there are certain problems. The entire rock is estimated to weigh around twelve tons, and in size alone it is too long for even the largest vehicle that El Paso can offer. It needs to be cut in half. Because Curt has been working for Bertha on her pottery from Las Madres—a project of hers apart from her museum duties—and because of my involvement with rock art, and because we are all a loosely affiliated group of interested parties, we become part of the rock-removal team. Curt enlists a friend with rock-cutting skills, to cut the stone in half, and we call on other friends to help with the complicated task of hoisting the desired piece onto the El Paso Gas truck. Bertha also recruits Walter Chappell, an internationally known professional photographer in Santa Fe, to document the entire process of moving the rock from Delgadito to its installation at the museum. Curt recalls that all those involved were hired for the job, although Walter was still negotiating with Bertha over his fees at the time the rock was hauled off. Bertha was tight with money.

In retrospect it is hard to contemplate just why we chose the last day of February near the end, but not *the* end, of a cold winter, to go after the rock. Part of it may have been enthusiasm for the enterprise and the prospect of a few extra dollars in the pocket, and part of it may have been because Curt had been hired as a seasonal ranger with the National Park Service that year (1966), and we were scheduled to go off to Navajo National Monument in mid-April. But we are all agreed, bored, and house-bound near the end of a long winter, that this is a great idea and we are off. "We" includes Curt and myself, plus three other families, Walter, and several family dogs. Among the ten children, several are only toddlers. We bring rock-cutting equipment, tipis, camping gear, and food for several days.

It is cold and damp in Delgadito.

We choose a nice sagebrush-covered flat for our camp. With some difficulty, a couple of tipis are pitched on frozen ground amidst the sage, a big campfire is built, and we settle in, a little down the canyon from the fallen ye'i rock.

The following morning while racing with exuberance across the frozen flat, I suddenly notice something ominous. It feels like I have a stake driven through my chest—something is really wrong. By the time breakfast is made I am trying to head off a sore throat with cups of hot coffee—to no avail, of course. There is an awful flu going around, and here I am being hit with it in this freezing camp. I can't recall much about what happened next, except that within a few hours, thoroughly fatigued, I took refuge in Walter's little tipi, which was decorated on the outside with designs in red and green. While the crew of guys was busy at the shelter and the sounds of rock saws and shouts echoed down the canyon, I huddled in my sleeping bag, trying to rest and stay warm. Walter, however, while mostly photographing the goings-on at the shelter, was in and out intermittently, stoking the fire inside the tipi. The fire, though welcome, was really smoky, the wood damp. I could hardly breathe even at ground level. In an effort to resolve the problem, I spent most of the day with my head outside under the edge of the tipi, the rest of me inside. That night, the three of us, Curt, myself, and Walter crowded inside, lanky Walter taking up most of the space. By morning I was much worse, and Curt decided I should be hauled out of there, and the Hadlocks who had visited the enterprise during the day, kindly welcomed me, evil viruses notwithstanding, to their house west of Farmington.

Meanwhile work on salvaging the rock had progressed. It had been cut in half, and the desired piece with most of the paintings was ready to be moved. But the beautiful Ghanskiddi, the mountain sheep deity, and Fringemouth ye'i that "had chosen" to remain on the cliff, spelled temptation for Kimmey, the stone mason, who argued that they should be removed and brought to Santa Fe to keep the group complete for the proposed exhibit. As a rational argument—that was one thing, but maybe something else was at work here—these were sacred paintings—maybe they had their own ideas about themselves. The Navajo say the spirit of the ye'i is invested in the image—were there other factors to consider beyond the geology of the rock that had cause these two to remain in place? A debate took place, and before leaving to drive me to Farmington, Curt told them to leave the remaining paintings alone. Period.

Kimmey had other ideas. What follows is what was reported to us later. In Curt's absence, they decided that they would try to remove the ye'i anyway. At the first blow of the hammer, an intense blast of snow and wind screamed down the canyon, and the camp was thrown into chaos amidst a spring squall. The kids screamed in fright, and the dogs barked. One dog, stranded high on a rocky ledge, howled to be rescued. That ended it. The ye'i on the cliff would remain in their canyon home—for now.

Soon after, the rock was loaded after countless problems in the wet mud and snow, all documented in dramatic footage. The truck, however, got hopelessly stuck, and a second truck had to be brought in to pull it out. The El Paso truck with its load, finally managed to spin and grind its way out of Delgadito and the Largo and head off to Santa Fe.

What happened right after that, I am too sick to care. The flu does not go away. The weather is damp, cold, cloudy and depressing. For a month—actually six weeks—I stagger around every day in our chilly three room house in Arroyo Hondo bundled up in long underwear and a heavy down jacket. I have various projects going on, papers to write. I am exhausted and can't manage much because of the toll the bug is taking on me. I eventually blame myself for this extreme fatigue. Self-blame is popular—it is all in your mind. A mantra common among our friends. I tell myself that if I can just get out of the house, pick up my notes and get myself down to Santa Fe and the Laboratory of Anthropology library where I can focus on other things, I'll get energized, I'll be okay. Curt and Dan Wolfman are planning to go to Albuquerque anyway to work on some computer stuff. I'll go along. I work all day in the library as congestion coursed through my respiratory system, and that evening Walter invites me to his and Nancy's house on Galisteo Street so that he can show me the footage he made of the Delgadito event. Ill, heavily congested (it seems to be getting worse) and exhausted I nevertheless agree. (The more mental diversion from my problems, the better, I think). The film is indeed spectacular. In the end, the sliding, the spinning wheels, the flying mud, and the anxiety about getting the big flat-bed semi with its precious load stuck and stranded made for a dramatic finale. I'm glad I hung in there—it may have been the only showing of that film seen by anyone beyond the Chappells. He and Bertha were at odds about the disposition of the film and payments he was owed, and the film was never finalized.

Marianne Wolfman, who had stayed in Santa Fe as well, and I are given refuge that night on Karl Kernberger's floor. The prospect of rest. A floor will do! When I wake up the next morning I have a sharp pain near my right side. What is this? I have no idea, but I do know that I want to just get home, and Marianne agrees to drive me the 80 miles back to Taos and Arroyo Hondo. Things are not going well. When we pass the medical clinic at Embudo I consider stopping, but the place is packed with cars—everyone in northern New Mexico is sick—at that point I lack the stamina to endure the waiting room. I would have to lie on the floor. No—keep driving. After delivering me to Arroyo Hondo, Marianne leaves but before she goes, at my insistence, she finds someone to stay and keep the fire going. Besides, I'm thinkng I might die. I'm afraid to be alone. By now, I'm coughing up blood and really scared. Curt is due home later that day.

By the time he arrives I'm begging to go to the hospital. X-Rays show my lungs full of crap that lead the doctor to decide that I have TB. They put me in a room with an old lady on her deathbed—the TB doesn't matter in that case. And then they run a test. Negative. Oh, you have pneumonia, they say. (I could have told them that.)

Despite what had developed into a long illness, with penicillin, I recover quickly, and within two weeks we are off to Arizona for the next six months.

Meanwhile, Bertha is obsessed with the desire to get those other two ye'i to Santa Fe before she has the exhibit built, and she hires someone for the plunder. The cliff where they once resided, today is scarred with deep permanent gouges, the ugly evidence of their forcible removal.

The exhibit was built as planned on the grounds of the Museum for Navaho Ceremonial Art. Several years passed. Karl was doing some photography for *The Indian Rock Art of the Southwest,* and I advised him that he could put off photographing the Delgadito Night Chant panel—still the very best known—until the last minute, since it was in Santa Fe and didn't require a field trip. But when he went to photograph it, he found that it was gone.

Unbeknownst to any of us, Bertha was gone too. It was 1975. Times were changing, and the new director felt "guilty" about having the museum possess sacred art, so at considerable expense he ordered the exhibit removed. The rock with its paintings was stored in a wooden crate somewhere. No one seemed to question whether or not *this* was ethical management of sacred art. Meanwhile, the Navajo tribe in Window Rock was planning to build a museum of their own, and the director in charge of the project wanted the rock. Shipped to Window Rock, it sat outdoors neglected. Plans for the new museum were stalled, and the funds reserved for the museum were redirected for sewers.

Several years after that a tribal museum was built, but by then it was too late. It was discovered that because the leaky crate with the ye'i images had been left out and forgotten in the weather, the paintings were all washed away. Only the finely incised lines of the feathers surrounding Ghanaskiddi's hump would have remained as faint testimony to what once was.

Or simply put, the ye'i left. They had had their revenge.

Hadlock later observed, with irony, that a huge boulder had fallen off the cliff on the opposite side of the canyon and landed near where our camp had been.

What became of the film documenting the drama of getting the rock remains a mystery. Thinking that the footage should at least still exist, following Bertha's death in 1994, at the invitation of her companion, Caroline Olin, we searched as the garage where her things were stored was cleared, hoping to find an old reel with the footage. Nothing turned up.

I then turned to Nancy Chappell, who was most helpful. Walter had since passed away as well, and she thought that the film might be found when their boys searched through his holdings. Nancy found some stills which she gave to me, but the film itself was missing.

In 1966 when the rock went to Santa Fe, the Bureau of Land Management (BLM), largely preoccupied with grazing rights, had little interest in their archaeological holdings. Although all that eventually changed, for years afterwards many people ascribed the deep gouges on the cliff at Delgadito were the work of random vandals—not knowing that the damage was done by a "paid vandal" under the auspices of a museum. The story of the Night Chant panel nearly vanished with the paintings themselves.

FAKE ROCK ART, OR IS IT?
by
Mavis Greer

The most common questions asked of rock art researchers are who made it and when. As comparative studies have progressed and new dating techniques have been developed, it's getting easier to answer those questions for many rock art panels. Of course, it has always been easier to answer it for some, such as scenes with horses in the Americas because the arrival date and spread of horses throughout the New World is known through other historical sources. However, there have always been rock art panels that have been hard to tie down, and this becomes more complicated when modern, non-Native American people make petroglyphs or pictographs that look like early American Indian rock art to intentionally mislead people or simply for the fun of it. In either case these situations cause problems for researchers and historic preservationists because soon people think they are ancient rock art images and when those who know differently die, it gets harder to prove who made them and when. Although with the right amount of time and money these modern panels can be revealed as such, many times those kinds of resources aren't available. Worse yet, as time goes by and stories about these sites become engrained in the folklore of the region, it becomes harder and harder to convince people of the truth. The best remedy is to make a record of a modern rock art site (or even just particular figures on a panel) as soon as possible and record the story associated with it such as Tom Kehoe did with a panel in Glacier Park, and so it is with the following places. (See "A Fraudulent Petroglyph from Glacier National Park," 1960, *Plains Anthropologist* 5:79-80. Thomas F. Kehoe.)

Of course, there are people that have placed names and dates on rock walls, either on earlier rock art or on clean surfaces, with no intention of it being mistaken for that of early people or cultures. These same people have occasionally left drawings of animals, plants, and even humans, but this kind of rock art is not meant to deceive or resemble early American Indian rock art and for the most part is easily identifiable. These people are leaving their mark for one reason or another, and it can be understood by looking at those drawings. For example, there is a site in southern Wyoming we call Justin's Wall. It is a small but prominent recessed area with nearly all inscriptions pertaining to Justin. At the top of the wall is: "To Justin My First Son," and beneath that the date "June 12, 1986"—presumably when the parent wrote the inscription as it was not Justin's birthdate because other inscriptions to and by Justin on this wall date earlier. Other inscriptions include "Hi Justin 1977; Hi Justin; Justin June 1989"; and a little sun figure with "Back Again, Hello Justin October 1978." Justin's Wall served as a message and memory bulletin board. It is not graffiti but instead honors Justin's life through the years. It provides a modern example of a rock art panel function that may also have implications for panels from the past.

This type of rock art is commonly termed graffiti. However, sometimes the term graffiti doesn't fit what we find, as Justin's Wall obviously served a purpose other than vandalism, which is usually associated with the term graffiti. Also, it is not "fake" rock art because it is not a forgery or a sham. There is a site in the wilds of northeastern Wyoming that has never been seen by a tourist and probably never will. In fact, the maker of the site undoubtedly never envisioned anyone but his (I feel fairly certain it was a young man based on the contents) friends seeing it as they were certainly the intended audience, although in some ways it appears almost a personal diary that no one was supposed to see. This rock art consists of drawings in addition to names and dates, but again it is not "fake" as it was not made by modern people to look like Native American Indian rock art that would fool someone. All of the modern images appear to be contemporary and include the name Casey and the year 2004. There is a marijuana plant, and a graphic sex scene labeled you and me, which lead us to refer to as the site as the Brokeback Mountain site since this content reminded us of the short story by Annie Proulx and subsequent movie. This panel was obviously made to commemorate an event important in the life of Casey.

We came upon the Brokeback Mountain site while surveying an access road to a planned well pad. A nice sandstone bluff beckoned to us, and we just knew there was rock art there. John got there first and saw the Casey panel. I arrived a little while later when the sun had changed positions a bit, and the first figure I saw was a large prehistoric shield, which is located away from the more deeply incised recent panel. The Casey panel maker probably never saw the early images and luckily did not carve over them.

Although the above sites are not "fake" rock art, there are panels that really are, where people made images that look so much like Native American Indian rock art that it will fool most who see it.

In 2002 a couple from Bozeman, Montana, contacted us to come and look at a new rock art site they had found west of town. We were excited to go as the site sounded like some other central Montana rock art we'd seen. They told us they were calling it the Secret Circle site as the paintings were on the wall at the entrance to an enclosed circular area with high rock formations. The location sounded like it perfectly fit the images, which were described as a line of humans with heads, necks, and long bodies but with no arms or legs. They described robed people like we'd recorded at other regional sites associated with ceremony, and the setting seemed to fit with a ritualistic function. It was a short hike from where we parked on the edge of a forest to the rock-enclosed circular conifer-filled area. We walked through a natural break in the rocks to enter the high boulder-lined circle, which hid any activities happening inside from the outside world, and we were sure this was an ancient ceremonial area. However, one look at the black charcoal-based painted figures on the wall extinguished our excitement for they had been painted on top of the growing lichen. They had been made to look like old central Montana pictographs, but they weren't. So, who made these and why? Although it could have been a tribal group replicating an old ceremony that included painting a line of humans, there is no other evidence of Native ritual enactments in this rock-enclosure. However, there was evidence of a recent partying with a firepit and alcohol. It could have been college students having fun and messing with people or it may have been new-agers conducting a ceremony that they formulated to copy an ancient one. Whatever the reason, the pictographs were not associated with an old Native American Indian activity.

Blacktail Cave is a real cave, not a rockshelter, along the Rocky Mountain Front in west-central Montana. This is a paleontological and archaeological site that's been known and worked for years. When John and I started intensively pursuing our rock art research interest in the region, many people asked us if we'd been to Blacktail Cave. When we said we hadn't, everyone told us we had to go there as it was not to be missed. So, we were anxious to see this cave with rock art, especially since rock art in the dark zone of caves is a special interest of ours and is something we hadn't seen in Montana and Wyoming caves. Even though the pictographs there were described as being in the entrance, not the dark zone, we thought if there are paintings associated with this cave, there is a good chance there may be rock art in the interior dark zone areas. However, even before we visited the cave, we heard rumors that the pictographs were not old but instead placed at the entrance to enhance the tourist value of the site.

Blacktail Cave is on a private dude ranch, so gaining permission to visit the site not as dude guests was a touchy situation, but after talking with the wife of the ranch couple, who told us that the pictographs looked much like those at the Dearborn River site in the region, we were granted permission to visit in 1992. We arrived at the ranch headquarters and talked a bit with the owners before heading out. Since the cave was used as a tourist attraction, there was a two-track road to the entrance, and we headed down that road to the site by ourselves. No one was at the cave, so we parked near the front and walked up an established trail with a wooden railing and over to a wooden ladder for a short climb down into the entrance. Once there we were pleased to see red pictographs that, like we had been told, were typical of the regional style.

The pictographs are in an alcove on a wall hanging from the ceiling right at the entrance. The entire panel is less than three-feet square and includes a variety of images including circles, dots, lines, a human hand, a bear paw, a bear, a stylized bird, a sun, and a large mask with a square face. We took photos of all the images, but felt the general appearance of some of the figures indicated that they were recently made, while others appeared to be older due to weathering, which we speculated may have been done artificially. Since there are known archaeological materials in the cave entrance alcove dating about 6000-6500 years ago while Pleistocene materials had been excavated farther in the interior, there was a possibility of the pictographs being authentic. So, if they were recently added, which we expected based on what we'd heard, they had to be copying other regional images.

Given the controversy surrounding these paintings, we knew it would be a good idea to date them to find out if they are modern or aboriginal, but there was no money or permission for this, so we needed to find clues to their age through other means. Blacktail Cave is a perfect example of why a site's recording history is invaluable. After visiting the site we began searching for who had visited the cave and when. We found that the paintings had been gradually added to the entrance over 20 years. Stuart Conner, a pioneer in Montana site recording, especially rock art, had been to the cave in 1960, and was emphatic that there was no rock art there, and this is a person with extensive experience in recognizing and recording rock art in the state. After talking with us, he looked through his photos and found one of him taken in front of the entrance in that year, and there were no paintings then. At the time we received the slide from Stu in the early 1990s there were no good enhancement computer programs, so it wasn't until 2018 when we were able to use DStretch on his photo to confirm no indications of even faded paint at the entrance that was no longer visible to the human eye. However, before that time we found other confirmation that the images were modern.

In the mid 1970s our brother-in-law, Tim Murphy, who was working as a fire fighter for the state of Montana visited the site. At that time he remembers seeing one red animal at the cave entrance, so it was after that time when other images were added so that by the 1990s paintings covered the entrance area. When we visited the cave again in 1996 Montana State University was digging in the cave interior. Dr. Leslie Davis was in charge of the excavations, and he knew a lot about the history of the cave. He was well aware that the pictographs in the entrance were late additions to the site. However, he was digging there with the blessing of the landowners, and he didn't want to cause any problems by reporting the pictographs were placed there to enhance tourism since everyone believed (especially the young agency archaeologists in the area) that they were authentic Native American Indian paintings. He did feel that the truth needed to be placed in the records for future researchers though, and he thought he would be the person to do it after he was finished with his work at the site because he had first hand knowledge of the situation. Also, he felt he could more diplomatically state it than anyone else who knew the history. We all agreed with him, and left it to Les. However, as fate would have it, he died before he was able to do this, so it is now left to us to set the record straight.

CONFRONTATION AT U-BAR CAVE
by
POLLY SCHAAFSMA

The woman on the other end of the line said that they had found "some things" in U-Bar Cave, and she thought the authorities should know about it so that the miners wouldn't get in trouble—she seemed worried. Curt, the State Archaeologist, was listening.

U-Bar Cave is a well-known archaeological site in the isolated country of the Chihuahua Desert in the bootheel of Hidalgo County, New Mexico. Unlike many so-called "caves" described in the archaeological literature of the American Southwest that are really open rock shelters, U-Bar is a dark cave, an ancient solution channel that runs back 315 feet into the limestone caprock of a fragmented mesa remnant northwest of the Alamo Hueco Mountains. Inside, the cave is 50 feet wide, and 23 feet high for much of its length, until it diminishes to 2 feet in height in the rear where it ends in several small grottos in a totally dark zone haunted by stalactites. Originally the opening at the mouth, some 400 feet above the valley floor, was small (4.5' high by 8' wide). Between 1976 and 1982 this was blasted open so that it could accommodate a D8 Caterpillar bulldozer for use in some early guano mining operations (see photo page 88). The depositional history of the deep bat guano and the question of several other entrances and their closures in the recent geologic past were later reviewed by biologist, Dr. Art Harris, who would be hired to conduct paleontological studies on the bones of the Pleistocene fauna contained in the deposits.

Directly below the cave is the Alamo Hueco Ruin, an Animas Phase site occupied between AD 1250 to 1400, with cultural ties to Casas Grandes in Chihuahua. Marge Lambert and Dick Ambler published an archaeological report on their work in the front the cave in 1965. Their findings, largely on the guano surface, included offerings that determined it had been a sacred location for the occupants of the site down below. By the time the archaeologists got there in the early 1950s, however, local ranchers had hauled away pottery and the prayer arrows from a shrine near the mouth. A photo of the shrine was subsequently illustrated by Lambert and Ambler, thanks to the locals who had had the foresight to photograph it before they made off with the contents.

The phone call in 1983 was precipitated by a renewed interest in the guano, and some miners had obtained a State Land Office permit to go after it, without consulting any archaeologists. In October Curt and I, with Bob Langsenkamp of State Land Office visited U-Bar, hiking in from the top of the ridge to evaluate the situation. We wanted to determine if there were further significant archaeological and/or paleontological materials remaining in the cave that would be impacted by removing the guano.

Inside it was really stinky, almost unbearably so. Millennia of bat droppings filled the bottom of the cave with deep guano, the undulating surface of which continued all the way to the dark reaches in the back. From the mouth ran a cable to which was attached a bucket that carried huge quantities of guano from the cave above to the bottom of the tramway. There was a flap in the bottom of this bucket that opened, so that the load could be released into a hamper, and then eventually transferred into sacks and put into trucks to be hauled away to buyers. Bats still occupied the cave, but the guano at the surface dated probably in excess of 5,000 to 10,000 years, and archaeological materials appeared to be limited to the surface and a few cracks and locations in the rear of the cave.

It was agreed that additional archaeological testing was in order. It seemed likely that more Animas Phase material remained in the cave, and there still existed the possibility that Paleoindian artifacts might turn up in deeper deposits in association with the Pleistocene fauna. Should this be the case, the site would be extremely unusual and significant to Paleoindian studies in North America. In light of these concerns, the land office attorney, Mr. Ray Leon, had visited U-Bar Cave and established a line beyond which the miners could not extract guano until further investigations could take place. At this point, all parties agreed to these official boundaries.

Thus it is, that in March 1984, Curt and I, with Walter Wait and George Haralson comprising a volunteer crew, arrive with our families at the U-Bar Ranch house. There we move our camping stuff and supplies into the functional, but somewhat dilapidated old place for a week's stay. The miners have stopped their digging and cleared out for the week, during which archaeological assessment will be conducted.

After a bumpy start on the archaeological end of things due to the politics involved, on Wednesday and Thursday Curt, Walter and Haralson work in the back of the cave where they find additional Animas Phase materials related to ritual offerings. Macaw feathers, colored cotton string, flower effigies, and a shell necklace are among the items collected on the guano surface.

Early Friday morning just as we are finishing breakfast, a belligerent, sassy, hot-tempered Mr. Louis Piper (a pseudonym) shows up at the ranch house wearing his hard hat—his identity symbol. He's the mining boss. Although expected, he was supposed to come alone, and we are not prepared for an invasion. Instead he has his entire crew in tow strutting around, including extra ammunition in way of the marketing supervisor of U-Bar Cave Products, who is anxious to maintain his guano sales contract. The day we arrived the miners had loaded 17 tons of guano in their semi at the bottom of the tramway. They are making a lot of money on the stuff, and it is rumored that it is being sold as super fertilizer for an illegal marijuana-growing operation in California. The miners feel that they have struck 'gold' and they have no intention of slowing down. These surly guys are in the mood for a fight.

Crowded together in the ranch house kitchen and now all ganged up, they demand permission to expand the pit, starting today. When it becomes apparent that there are still restrictions on where they can mine guano, Piper calls his lawyer on the ranch phone. When he hangs up, in response, Curt calls his. Curt, anticipating this, had previously contacted the attorney at the State Land Office, Bill Garcia, in Santa Fe who naively told Curt to not let them expand the pit and to control them by reference to the state law. Should they exceed the established boundaries, they would be subject to criminal proceedings. Hardly helpful, this so-called threat elicits mocking laughter. It is clear that back-up is in order. Curt is now requesting that Garcia have the State Police in Deming call the ranch so that he can arrange a police escort to accompany him to the cave. It is likely that the miners will do as they please and expand the pit once they get up there.

In response and unwilling to take any action, the deputy Land Commissioner in Santa Fe was reluctant to ask the State Police to drive to the ends of the earth into the far reaches of the bootheel, and he decided that it would be much easier to simply arrange a Conference Call with all involved, during which Piper would be "forced" to agreed not to dig guano beyond the established limits. Of course, an agreement was reached to work things out amicably—you can say anything on the phone.

How effective will this be?

On Saturday morning, Piper tells Curt he is returning with his crew to sack the guano they had accumulated at the base of the tramway last week. With no one in the cave, this will give Curt a chance to return to tidy up his notes, take photos, and make some final profile drawings. And meanwhile, Art Harris and his students are scheduled to arrive and take over the scientific operations beyond the pit. When Curt arrives at the base of the tramway, he discovers that Piper has put his men to work again in the cave digging guano, and that Piper is running the tram. With a sinister grin he gleefully offers Curt a ride up to the cave in the bucket. Figuring that Piper planned to open the bucket half way up, dumping him out, Curt declines, preferring to climb. Upon arrival at the cave, he discovers Piper's crew working furiously, digging beyond the established boundaries, and greatly expanding the pit. As Curt wrote:

"I expected to find them working within the limits of the pit working only in the deposits at the bottom...I was quite unprepared to find that they had greatly expanded the pit to the to the east, north, and west...they were working furiously with 2-3 people shoveling in the pit and 4-5 people carrying guano to the tram in the wheelbarrow." (Curt's field journal, March 24, 1984).

Their tale about sacking bags of guano had been a lie.

As planned, shortly Art arrives with his students, and Curt turns any further work there over to him. A monitor provided by the mining company will keep the miners in line during Art's excavations that will be focused on finding bones of Pleistocene fauna. If archaeological materials were to be found that required excavation, we will be notified.

As he leaves, Curt is still apprehensive about Art missing any of the subtle indications of a Paleoindian presence such as small lithics. Should there be any, U-Bar Cave could turn out to be a major early man site, but nothing of that nature was ever reported. Harris later published his findings on the bones.

And we never did learn anything about "the things" the miner's wife was concerned about.

INDIAN COUNTRY, HAIGHT-ASHBURY, AND THE UTE CHAINING PROJECT

by

POLLY SCHAAFSMA

We pack up the boys, dogs, our black cat Coca-lola, ourselves, and camping gear into our new pickup and head off to the Mountain Ute Reservation on the south side of the Mesa Verde in southwestern Colorado. It is the summer of 1967, and the Utes are planning to chain down the piñon pines and junipers across the mesa top in an effort to grow more grass and thus increase the tribe's grazing potential. The mesa is peppered with Pueblo archaeological sites, and it is our job to make surface collections of the sherds and lithics we encounter as we walk the terrain designated for chaining. We are to tie pink flagging tape around the sites, to prevent the chaining operation from ripping them up and destroying their archaeological value. When on survey we also tie pink flagging tape on our two boys so that we won't lose them in the thick woods.

Our contract is for two months work. The boys and I are just 'along for the ride.' Hoski, seven, plans to hike with the crew all day, but Pieter is only three years old, and we will spend afternoons at leisure in camp or on the mesa close to where the men are surveying.

Mike Marshall and David MacNeece have been hired as part of the team. We have a state vehicle and a small camping trailer, and Curt and I have our own tipi. As the survey moves across different parts of the mesa top, we move our camp accordingly. The archaeological survey is required by law, but this was not the first attempt to carry it out.

There have been problems. All of the Utes are not agreed among themselves that outsiders should even be allowed on their land, and we are—well, at least vaguely—aware of this problem. Back in 1955 when he was a teenaged summer employee at the Mesa Verde Company in the national park, Curt had had a personal encounter with a Ute with a rifle. He had been warned by a ranger and knowledgeable local not to venture beyond the park boundaries as the Utes were hostile to trespassers. It was said that trespassers had been known to vanish. This piece of knowledge was just what motivated a then seventeen-year-old Curt to give it a try, so he made a day hike down to the Mancos River Canyon that bisects the mesa. On his return up Soda Canyon he saw a Ute with a rifle tracking him on horseback. The walls of Soda are steep and formidable with limited points of access to the mesa top, but somehow Curt managed to elude his pursuer and escape up some crack in the cliffs. Not knowing any of this, a week later I, also a Mesa Verde Company employee, made the same hike with a clueless park ranger, but luckily we encountered no one.

To our naive young minds, the twelve years that had elapsed between 1955 and 1967 seemed like a half-century. Surely things would have changed by now. A whole decade and more had passed, and the inevitable inroads of civilization would have dispelled all possibilities of wild hostilities. And besides, we were so jubilant about the opportunity to spend two months on Mesa Verde that we didn't give potential threats like this much thought.

But there were warnings, nevertheless. The previous year in 1966, the University of Colorado had contracted to do the work we were now faced with, and Bruce Anderson had been the person in charge of the survey. In an account he later delighted in telling, he had been caught and held captive by the Utes who drove him off the mesa to their headquarters in Towaoc with a pistol jammed into his ribs. At that point Colorado scrapped the deal. The following year the Laboratory of Anthropology at the Museum of New Mexico in Santa Fe picked up the contract, and Curt accepted the project. To avoid a repeat of armed confrontation, Curt has hired two Ute guys, Fred and Wilson to assist on the survey. They don't camp with us but commute everyday from Towaoc.

Life on the mesa is working out very well. Our camps on the edges of the piñon-juniper woods, scheduled for destruction, of course, are pleasant, wild, and isolated. In fact, our nice two dogs take note of this, and after only about a week their eyes begin to glaze over when they look at us. They stare blankly before racing off to chase rabbits, rustle up lizards and whatever else dogs will do when on their own more or less in remote places like this. They begin to stay away for long interludes, and we are becoming a little concerned when one day, we notice Tooki Ta-a and Chica racing into our camp with a coyote buddy in tow, all apparently heading for the food dish that we keep available for them. Needless to say, in the interest in keeping our beloved dogs, we henceforth manage their habits more closely.

Among the amenities that we enjoy—or attempt to enjoy—after hot days of hiking, is a battery-operated record-player. It cranks out the latest acid rock emanating from the counter-culture hippie movement that far beyond us at this very moment is flooding the country in the big cities. It is said that right now the scene in San Francisco is reaching a peak. And we vicariously tune in on Janis Joplin, Big Brother and the Holding Company, the Beatles, and Jefferson

Airplane, listening over and over to songs belted out by great singers, but digested and regurgitated in diminished form by David's machine. The music really is not sounding very good.

Suddenly it is the Fourth of July, and we have four days off and nothing to do. We can choose to work but our Ute companions want the break. We can return to our homes in New Mexico, but with nothing in particular to do there either. Then someone comes up with the bright idea that if we jump to it *right now immediately—say within the next ten minutes* we have just time enough to drive to Haight-Ashbury at its peak. It's "The Summer of Love" in San Francisco, and to be able to say that we had been there—"What a great story to tell our grandchildren!" they—Mike, David, and Curt—exclaim.

I disagree. The thought of a hot, crowded, beeline trip to San Francisco appalls me. I object. I say no.

The mood in camp plunges. Mike and David walk around sulking. Curt, also sulking, doesn't have anything to say. Only the kids and dogs don't care, but that hardly makes up for the resentment being expressed by everyone else. Being Poison Polly quickly—probably within 15 minutes—becomes unbearable. I give in.

If we are going to do this crazy thing, we have to leave—now! Curt, myself, Mike and David squeeze into the front of our pickup along with our black kitty, Coca-Lola. With the boys and our two dogs in back, we drive off the mesa, head west through Mancos Canyon and 'Indian country" and out toward San Francisco.

However, we we don't have a good idea of how to get there. We plan to drive all night in the right direction—West. We don't take time to look at a map (I doubt that we even had one) and choose a good route, so we just drive toward the setting sun. There is no I-70 yet and Route 66 is too far south—or so it seems. By the time we reach Green River, Utah we are low on gas and being late, there are no open gas stations. We drive on to Bicknell where we actually run out of gas and our only choice is to park there until they open up in the morning. Maddening delay. But morning finally arrives, we fill the tank, and on we go, twisting endlessly along mountain roads, progressing much too slowly across Utah, then through wide Nevada, passing the waving cowboy on the strip in Reno, and finally into California.

Our immediate plan is to head to Curt's mother's (Trudy) house in Vallejo where we will leave her to mind her grandsons, the dogs, and cat, while we run off to the Big City to have fun. We must have called ahead because when we arrive, Trudy has a big meal ready and also a lecture. "I hope you kids aren't planning to go over to San Francisco" she tells us. It is a severe warning. "They say everybody's on drugs and things are really crazy over there right now and it is dangerous." After the usual pleasantries, we assure her that going to San Francisco is exactly what we have in mind. Trudy wasn't stupid. I'm sure she had it all figured out before we even got there.

Haight Street is bustling with a milling mob, and hippie businesses lining the streets are thriving. For sale everywhere is an issue of *The Oracle*—just out and now famous—a hippie newspaper, lauding the values of Native Wisdom and Indian Country. We feel really special having just arrived from Real Indian Country with the dust of Mesa Verde and the reservation still on our clothes and in our hair. A jewelry merchant asks us where we are from and when we say "Taos", he acknowledges that he knows two people from Taos—Kathleen Summit and Emil Pfeiffer. We assure him that we know both, because we do, and that makes us feel even more at home on Haight Street. Everyone knows someone who knows someone, and everybody seems to be connected.

Afternoon brings the music—live—our original excuse for coming. Big Brother and the Holding Company and a bunch of other bands are holding forth on Mount Tamalpais with Janis Joplin belting out her songs. The crowd is enormous. We dance to rock all afternoon under the eucalyptus trees until the whole thing breaks up, and people by the thousands start streaming down the mountain. We have in mind seeking out our friend Alice in Bolinas, but we have no idea where in Bolinas she is or even how to go about finding her. We understand she's camping in the woods somewhere. Meanwhile in our truck we creep through crowds of people asking for rides, and we pick up at random a young girl wearing beads and a headband. When we ask where she is going, she simply answers that she was going to see Alice. *Our* Alice?—Yes, Alice Lane—Incredible! We tell her that we are going to see Alice too, but we don't know how to find her, and this hippie chick takes us right to the camp where Alice is living with her boyfriend in a lean-to. Meanwhile, this new 'friend,' intrigued by our stories wants to come back to Mesa Verde with us and learn all about archaeology in real "Indian Country." She is, naturally, very enthusiastic, and assures us that she can pack up and be ready in no time. This does not bode well for camp harmony however. Fortunately there is one hitch to this bright idea of bringing a 'souvenir' plaything (remember, this is the sixties) from Mount Tam back to our camp—she was told she must get my permission.

I say "no," and this time I mean it.

Our return to Mesa Verde is more direct. We stick to Route 66—or maybe it was I-40 by then. Whatever, no matter, it is fast, straight, and hot. In the Mohave desert our poor little cat starts to pant, fade, and become limp. We stop in Amboy—nearly a ghost town—and find a fast food joint open, buy a Coke, and save the ice in a towel which we then wrap around Coca-Lola, and hold the chilly bundle out the window as we drive. She recovers, quickly, thankfully. After a long night, we reach our camp on the mesa at sunup, just in time to go to work. Fred and Wilson arrive too, just as we pull in. Utterly wiped out, we tell them to come back tomorrow, and we head for bed.

One evening after our return and after Fred and Wilson leave for the day, Mike finds a stash of juniper logs he is interested in, so he goes off to chop them into smaller pieces. Meanwhile a group of Utes, the first we've seen besides our fellow surveyors, have moved a herd of cattle upslope from our camp, and they, too, have set up a tipi and are making camp nearby. When they hear someone chopping wood, they drive over to investigate in a big cattle truck. It slowly rattles to the edge of our camp and stops. We stop too. Tense, I sit with our boys and hold onto the dogs, as Curt walks over to "see what they want." Ha! They demand to know what we are doing on their land, of course. As Curt stands by their truck, we watch in stony silence as the man in the passenger seat slides a long a rifle barrel out the window into Curt's face. I am just far enough away that I can't hear what is being said, but the conversation is really lengthy, and I'm getting nervous and the gun never moves. I am hoping that they might notice the children—that might cool them off. Curt offers to show them our papers, proving that we are there legally and all, but they could care less about papers. They've got him at gunpoint and they are in control. At long last and after endless talk, and ultimately saved by mention of Fred and Wilson, the rifle barrel slowly moves back, and they start their truck and rumble off. The next day they move their herd, and we never see them again. Yes, it is still 'Indian Country'.

Morning coffee, Delgadito camp, March 1, 1966. Standing, Carol Hinton with Miles; seated left to right: John Kimmey, Steve Hinton with Jesse, Curt Schaafsma with Pieter, and Polly with coffee. (Photograph by Walter Chappell, courtesy of Polly Schaafsma)

Tipis at Delgadito camp.
(Photograph by Walter Chappell, courtesy of Polly Schaafsma)

Curt, Harry Hadlock, and
Hoski Schaafsma examining
underside of the fallen slab with
paintings, October 1965.
(Photograph by Polly
Schaafsma)

Holy People of the Night Chant group before the collapse.
(Photograph by Harry Hadlock, courtesy of Polly Schaafsma)

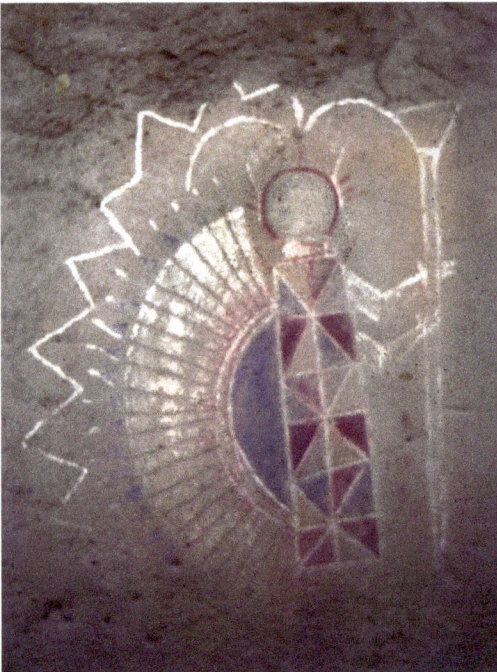

Splendid Humpback God, leader of the Night Chant panel. Incised and painted in red, white, azurite blue, orange and turquoise
(Photograph by Harry Hadlock, courtesy of Polly Schaafsma)

Night Chant panel installed on the grounds of at the Museum of Navaho Ceremonial Art in Santa Fe, in the 1970s. (Photograph by Polly Schaafsma)

Justin's Wall (48CR9619) in south-central Wyoming; inverted enhancement. (Photograph by Mavis Greer)

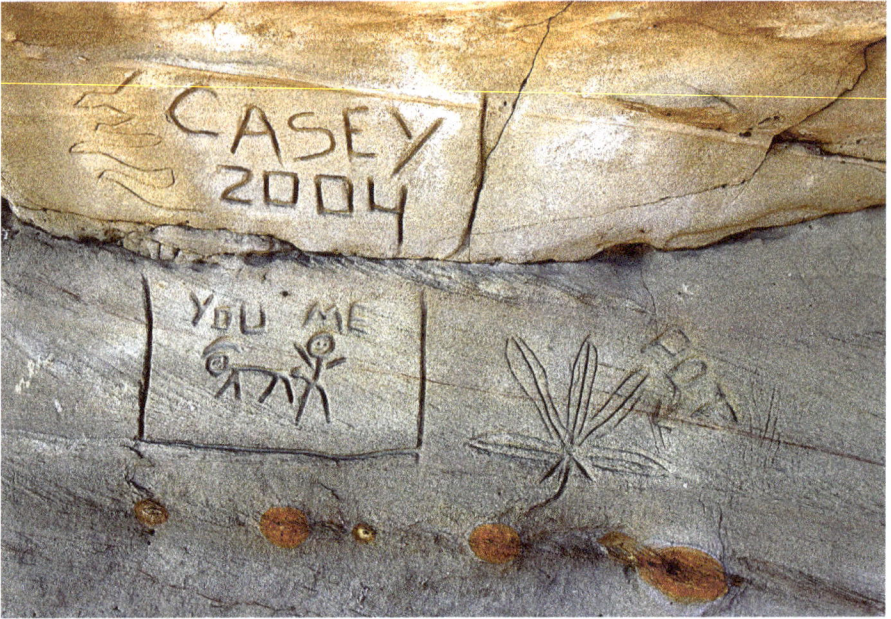

Casey Wall at the Brokeback Mountain site (48CA6177) in northeastern Wyoming. (Photograph by John Greer)

Aboriginal shield at the Brokeback Mountain site (48CA6177) in northeastern Wyoming. (Photograph by John Greer)

Human figures at the Secret Circle in southeastern Montana. (Photograph by John Greer)

View of the approach to the main entrance into Blacktail Cave (24LC151), 1992; John is standing at the entrance. (Photograph by Mavis Greer)

Mavis at the main entrance into Blacktail Cave (24LC151), 1992.
(Photograph by John Greer)

Pictographs in the main Blacktail Cave (24LC151) entrance, 1992.

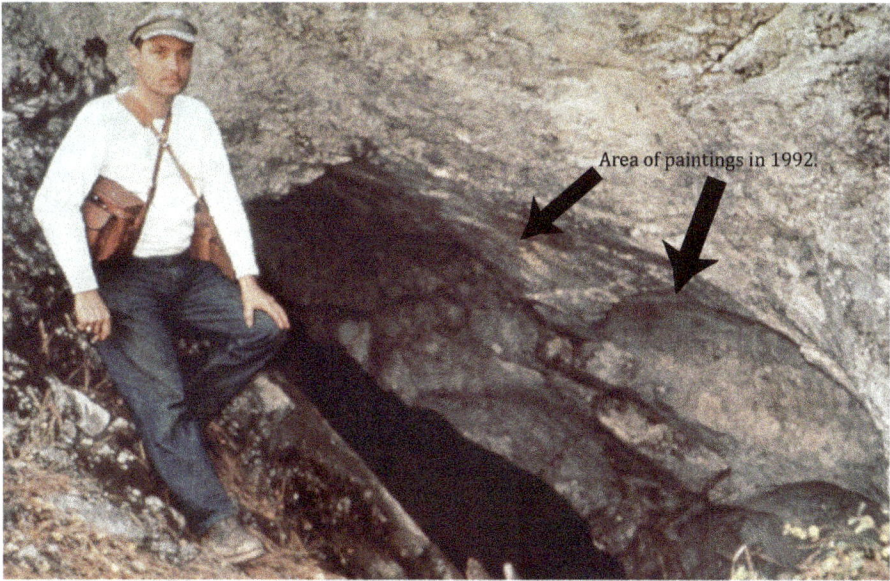

Area of paintings in 1992.

Stuart Conner in the same entrance to Blacktail Cave (24LC151) in 1961 as shown in INSERT 63. Note the lack of paintings in 1961. (Photograph courtesy of Stuart Conner)

View west/southwest from U-Bar Cave in the bootheel, Hidalgo County New Mexico, 1984. Note the high cable. (Photograph by Curtis Schaafsma)

Excavating in the bat guano in the dark rear of U-Bar Cave.
(Photograph by Curt Schaafsma)

6
RIGHT PLACE AT THE WRONG TIME

Mavis at the small entrance into Surratt Cave, New Mexico.
(Photograph by John Greer)

ON THE WRONG END OF A LAWSUIT
by
Mavis Greer

It was not like other contract surveys from the beginning. For one thing it was on the Crow Reservation in southeastern Montana, and it involved getting a permit from the Bureau of Indian Affairs (BIA), which meant extra time and work. However, that process went smoothly, and we were ready to proceed with the archaeological survey of six coalbed methane wells. One permit stipulation was that we were to be accompanied to the field by two members of the Crow tribe, so we coordinated our schedules and were ready to go to the field in early November 1999. One of the six wells was on private surface with Crow-owned minerals, so prior to going out we contacted the landowner via phone. John made the call and talked with the ranch wife (I'll call her Ethel), who gave us permission to be at the planned well pad on that day.

It was a nice fall day, and we were only surveying small areas around each of the staked well pads, so we were moving along nicely. The two tribal members were a woman (I'll call her Jane) with extensive knowledge of the laws concerning all things oil and gas and cultural resources on Indian lands, and a man (I'll call him Joe), who was roped into coming along with her that day since the cultural resource specialist for the tribe was sick, and their policy for safety was always to have at least two people on a job. They were helpful in knowing the local area, and we followed them from one well to the next. At the wells they sat in their pickup while we did the survey, and then we were off to the next well. We saved the one on the private ranch until last, so it was in the afternoon when we made the trip to the east side of the reservation. We entered the well by driving past the ranch house and traveling down a well-used two-track.

As we drove down the two-track following the tribal pickup, we heard the roar of a large pickup coming up behind us and driving at a rapid rate of speed. The next thing we know, the pickup is passing us on the right as it bounces across the sage. It gets between our pickups and drives in a caravan with us to a wire gate in the fence. As we all stop for the fence, Jane, who is in the front vehicle, gets out to open the gate. At the same time the rancher (I'll call him Fred) gets out of his pickup obviously beyond outraged, scaring us all. John and I then also got out, as did Joe. The first thing Fred said is, pointing to us "you have permission to be here" and pointing to Jane and Joe, "you don't." At that point Jane, who was at the gate, began quoting laws that allowed them to be there, but Fred wasn't listening as he became more and more enraged and belligerent.

At this point the words being said are lost to me as Fred starts getting in Joe's face. John is also chiming in trying to cool Fred down and explain the situation. In the meantime, I pass through the gate and begin doing the survey in an effort to avoid the confrontation and do the work, so we won't have to come back here. Back at the fight, Fred and Joe are near coming to physical blows, although no hitting was ever done, and are moving away from the pickups out into the open sage area. I happen to look over just as Fred backs up into a sage and falls. Never during the entire confrontation did any fists fly, but there was a lot of shouting and pushing. However, the fall taken by Fred was not due to pushing but due to his not paying attention to where he was going and "yelling while walking." After the fall, John and Joe reach down to pull Fred to his feet and find he has broken his leg at the hip bone. Fred is a big guy, and it takes both of them to get him to his pickup. Once there it's obvious that he can't drive, so they put him in the passenger side. While this is going on, Jane comes over to talk with me. She asks if they should just leave, and I agree that's the best thing to do as we can take care of getting Fred home. Once Fred is in the pickup, Jane gets Joe, and they drive through the gate onto Crow land with the intention of following two-tracks to better roads to avoid going by Fred's house.

John then gets into Fred's pickup to drive it back to his house while I drive ours there. Once at the house, Ethel comes running out to find out what's wrong, and once she knows, she calls 911. While waiting for the ambulance, Fred gets out of the pickup and stands leaning against the seat. We all gather round him and make small talk as we wait and wait and wait. In the meantime, Ethel calls her son, who is with the sheriff's office in Sheridan, Wyoming, and he says he is on his way. After waiting for some time, she realizes that her 911 call went to Hardin, Montana, which is some distance away but the county seat for their ranch, and not to Sheridan, Wyoming, which is the closest town. This is then remedied, and soon after that the ambulance from Sheridan arrives. Fred is loaded in the ambulance, and Fred and Ethel's son, who is there by this time, and we follow it to town.

At the hospital, we hear that a Big Horn County sheriff deputy is on his way down to interview us about the fight, so we wait to talk with him. When he arrives, it is the second in charge as the sheriff is a tribal member, and they wanted someone who wasn't to talk to Fred and Ethel, who were not tribal members, and to us. John and I were interviewed separately. After telling the story as I remembered it, the deputy asked me if I was afraid during the confrontation, and

I told him absolutely. I was just hoping no guns would come out. He wanted to know whom I was afraid of, and I told him Fred...he was beyond out of control. The deputy told us that when Jane and Joe arrived back in Crow Agency, they had gone immediately to the BIA and reported the incident, which as it turned out was a big help to us.

Well a month or so went by, and one day we were in the area of the ranch, so we stopped by to see how Fred was doing. He was much better, back at home, and in a much better mood than when we'd last seen him. We left there thinking all was fine with him and that the incident was only a memory...wrong.

Shortly after our visit we receive a notice that Fred and Ethel filed suit on us for Trespassing and were seeking $750,000 in restitution. We are like...are you kidding! Well, obviously it was not a joke, so we immediately contacted our insurance agent. After years and years of Business Liability Insurance payments, we found ours was about to pay off big time. Our agent was comforting and assured us that they would take care of it. However, taking care of it involved a lot of time from us as we had to prove we had contacted them before going to the well (we had telephone records for that), we had to prove that we had been authorized by the oil company to provide the survey on their behalf (we had emails for that), and we had to make a deposition to lawyers in Billings, which was the location of the jurisdiction court. Our insurance company had hired a law firm out of Billings to handle our case, and when we got there to meet our lawyer our first impression was not exactly comforting. He looked about 15 years old, but he was a recent graduate of the University of Montana law school, and we were his first case. It turned out that this was a good thing since he really, really wanted to win and prove to his new law firm that he was a worthy employee.

It was during the deposition we heard that Fred was already in a lawsuit with the Crow tribe over some land boundaries, so he did not want to or could not sue them again. He had tried to sue the oil company, but they got it dismissed because we were a third party operating on their behalf. So, their last resort to get money from the fight was us, and since neither John nor I were involved in the fight, he had no reason to sue other than a made up trespass charge. It was during this deposition that we learned that the paperwork filed by Jane and Joe at the BIA the evening of the confrontation stated that Fred's first words when he got out of the pickup about us were "you have permission to be here." That, and the phone and emails records, meant his lawsuit was a lost cause. In fact, it was only a few weeks later that our insurance company informed us that the judge had dismissed the case. However, it cost our insurance company $32,000 to fight this lawsuit. The moral of the story is...never run a business without liability insurance. You never know when a lawsuit will come out of left field.

FLOATING ON THE SURFACE OF XIBALBA: SAVED BY A STRING ON THE USUMACINTA

by

POLLY SCHAAFSMA

Frontera Corozal, Chiapas, October 1992: I'm sitting on a crate on a muddy bank at the edge of a funky town watching the wide silver surface of the Rio Usumacinta rush past, while a team of guys loads the rubber rafts with camping gear and several days' worth of food. It has been two days since we left Palenque and the motel Xibalba, the name of which refers to the watery Maya Underworld, the abode of the Lords of Death. This river trip is the highly anticipated focus of our venture into the rainforests of southern Mexico and Guatemala. We will float on the surface of Xibalba, we joke. No one cares that it is the rainy season with daily deluges and oppressive humidity. Armed with Deet and fully clothed against the attacks of armies of mosquitos, we've been suffering these little inconveniences for several days. The exhausting heat and nuisance of the bugs are overridden by the spectacular Maya ruins at Palenque, the sounds of howler monkeys and the excitement of meeting the Lacandones who inhabit these regions and offer us beautifully carved wooden spoons for purchase.

No one cares that it is the height of the rainy season because it is the off-season for river guides up north where we've come from and for guides on the Usumacinta as well, who limit their tours to the dry months of the year. Being free from work on the San Juan River in Utah, and looking for off-season possibilities elsewhere, Charlie Delorme, owner of Wild River Expeditions in Bluff, has organized this little exploration party to see if he can contemplate future trips to Maya ruins on the Usumacinta while it snows up north.

We are a varied group. Along with Charlie, his crew includes Tamara Wiggans, Red Wolf (also known as Colorado), Doug Ross, Tom, Stephanie, and another river guide named Dan. And finally, there is a couple from Durango, Colorado who during the winter months make their headquarters in Palenque and work as guides on the Usu—our affectionate nickname for this river. The Durango couple, I'll call them Matt and Celia, "know" the river—at least when it's not in flood—and their knowledge of places along the way will be useful as well. In addition there are several "guests", some of whom are archaeologists—myself and Curt, Al Hayes and his wife Karen, Mark Michaels, who is the director of The Archaeological Conservancy, and Doug's girlfriend, Carla.

The muddy water moves swiftly, filling the broad expanse of the channel bank to bank. I recall having seen photographs from National Geographic in which banks and rocky cliffs 50 feet or more in height were exposed above the river below the edge of the rain forest. The tree line was determined by annual high water levels below which nothing grows, and today the edge of the water brushes the trees. We will travel fast down this watery avenue that separates Mexico from Guatemala.

Our immediate destination is the site of Yaxchilan, where we plan to spend a day or two exploring before reaching the remote site of Piedras Negras on the Guatemalan side. No one says anything about the river but when we get to Yaxchilan, Matt expresses some astonishment about the fact that his familiar camping spot is submerged and that we have to dock against the vegetation and make a difficult ascent up a bank before reaching the level of the ruins. It is dusk on our arrival. We enter the site through a little, dark, walled passageway. Doug sticks his hand into a wall niche and discovers a small wiggly snake. Careful—this is Fer-de lance country—luckily, it doesn't bite him.

Our camp has the benefit of a large shelter that keeps us 'dry'—now a relative term—but out of the evening rains. By this time, a couple of the 'guests' are suffering severely with red welts all over their legs for having scorned the need for long pants. Long pants tucked securely into one's socks are the only thing that works. We examine the carved lintels, and study maps and drawings from Schele and Friedels' *Forest of Kings* to better understand this now seemingly enchanted place where in the old days ballgame losers were rolled into a ball and thrown down long temple stairways, all illustrated in the lintel carvings by the victors. Photos of our company taken by Karen show us as a wilted group above Structure 33, the grand temple with its a lovely high roof comb at the summit of a hill. One evening we even have a little jungle birthday party, complete with cards and a cake and everything when I suddenly become a year older. Even here there is no escape from time's passing. Howler monkeys howl about the futility of it all, but somehow we are content.

Down the river we pass an ejido called El Cayo, and women and children stare at us from the bank. Matt with his acquired wisdom explains that this is not a good place to stop even though there is a site nearby. The farming occupants of the settlement, moved in from elsewhere in Mexico, are said to be hostile. In fact, a few years later they attacked some archaeologists with rocks, who escaped on foot via the river (not in the rainy season). The archaeologists, realizing that a sculpted altar there was endangered, were interested in acquiring it for a museum.

The new locals were threatened by this because they wanted to sell it.

We float past.

The river becomes wider and ever more powerful. I try my hand in a rubber ducky, one of the small one-person boats brought along for the adventurous. I really don't like much being seated so close to the water, and after a while the strong currents of the river get to me. Yes, the surface of this muddy creek is not flat, but it flows in uneven ridges, possibly reflecting a rough riverbed, and there is the creepy feeling that Xibalba is too close to the surface. Beneath me, it seems, is this powerful serpent that could unexpectedly carry me off far from the other boats. Or flip me over. Feeling powerless and slightly panicked by the thought that I might not be in control, I return to the big rubber raft.

Down river, hills covered with rain forest growth rise up, enclose us on both sides. We laze along we watch pairs of scarlet macaws chattering, conversing with each other overhead as they cross the river. White hawks startle us with their bright contrast against the greenery, and the wavering moaning of unseen howler monkeys becomes the background voice of the jungle wilderness itself— everything in harmony.

On toward the mysterious site of Piedras Negras.

Piedras Negras is named for some big black rocks on the beach below the ruins, or so we are told. Being high water, of course we never see this nice beachy place with the famed rocks. Once again we have to negotiate a steep vegetated bank, and this time we camp on a narrow slope at the foot of a trail into the forest that leads into the ruins, now mostly hidden under a sea of green foliage. All four rafts are secured by a single composite rope arrangement. Celia, super-river guide that she is, had tied the knots. I grow uneasy—to Celia's complete disgust. Why is everything hitched with a single tie rope. What if something chews the rope— Then what? We are in Guatemala, and guerilla hideouts could be anywhere. It is not safe should we need to exit by land. And how would we do that anyway? My mind is in overdrive.

I have to put my useless fears aside. Forget tomorrow. Right now we are here at the famous site of Piedras Negras after all. We find a tiny path that soon joins another slightly larger path leading to the ruins. We pass a tractor abandoned there following a University of Pennsylvania expedition the 1930s. The tractor is rusted and covered with brilliant green moss. How did they get it here anyway? Nearly completely hidden, submerged in the forest, are the limestone blocks of the structures themselves peeking out at us from the under a lush green leafy blanket. The hollow eyes and mouth of the famed "monkey face" stares out from under moss and ferns. The trail is small, half obliterated by plants. Daylight wanes. As everyone returns to our camp, Curt and I lag slightly behind, when we see a huge Ceiba tree straight in front of us that we have not encountered before. This is not good. Obviously we are in the wrong place on a different trail. Whose trail is this?

Where does it go, we wonder? Maybe we are not far from camp. So we yell. We receive an answer. Thank god! We've missed the obscure little passage branching off to our camp that joins the one we are on, a junction we never noticed earlier.

Back on track we pass by our tents, lined up nicely on the side of the sloping path to the "camp kitchen." Against the green of the rain forest, they form a pretty line of bright colors like a display in a sporting goods store. Except that it isn't. Before nightfall closes in, a community of army ants establishes its route across the foot trail and up over Charlie's tent. The loo or "groover" as it was known—due to the linear impressions created on one's hinder from sitting on the hard-edged big plastic bucket—a problem resolved by the simple addition of toilet seat—is set up on the other side of the army ants' highway. Being the last tent in line means that we will have to jump carefully over this traffic should any need occur in the middle of the night. Que complicacion!

As for tent-living in the rain forest, Curt and I have established a routine. Of course, the tent is always zipped tight. After we set it up, we crawl inside fast, zip up again, and then proceed to empty our rubber river bag of its few contents that include sleeping bags and a small amount of clothing. We then grab the socks, shirts, and underwear, unzip the door, crawl outside, zip up again and then proceed to string the items along the rope along the top of the tent. The purpose of this ritual is not to dry things out—it might rain during the night anyway—but simply to air the stuff to keep it from stinky mildew. It seems to work. At the end of the trip, Curt discovers his leather belt, neglected, coiled up in the bottom of the bag covered with a healthy coat of green mold.

Meanwhile I'm suffering somewhat—it could be worse—but it is slightly problematic nevertheless—from the usual—Montezuma's revenge. We've been asleep only a short while when I have to make the dreaded hike to the groover. Curt comes with me. With our flashlights we find and jump over the still active interstate of marching army ants. My god, it is black in the forest. The second time I need to get up, we decide to go up the trail and skip the loo and the ants. We repeat this act a third time. The fourth time I assure Curt I can handle this by myself and go it alone through the impenetrable darkness with one flashlight. In the forest canopy above, the moaning howl of monkeys adds an eerie note to my short solo foray. About five seconds after I click off my light, heavy foot falls stomp past me not six feet away. I can see nothing. It can only have been a person. Are we being watched? Who made the trail by the Ceiba tree? Startled, I straighten up, fully recovered by fear, and hurry back downhill to our tent.

There are answers to these questions. In the morning while our merry crew is drinking coffee and feasting on cereal, eggs, and tortillas, three armed men burst into camp—an older man, his grown son, and his kid about 10 or 12 years old. Here are the famed and feared guerillas right here in our kitchen, all carrying rifles. Oh Happy Day!

"*Muy Buenos Dias*. The boaters speak Spanish well and welcome this gun-toting army of three with happy smiles as if they are resurrected Maya royalty. Hot coffee is graciously served by Tamara and Celia. The guerillas relax, and so do we. Finally the elder man, standing, gives a long oration in Spanish, explaining who they are and how they are protecting their land and lives against the cruel hand of an unjust government. We all nod and agree enthusiastically throughout his articulate formal speech. And at the end, to our relief, he tells us that it is okay that we are camped at Piedras Negras because archaeological sites are public places and we are safe here. We show our appreciation with copious gifts of coffee and chocolate, they pick up their guns, retreat up the trail and disappear.

Our focus now is on is on the river.

The boats are secure and being loaded. The rope did not get chewed by an animal! But unlike the previous days on the river, we face some uncertainties. We will never know what Matt—our person with access to the local tales knew at that point—but we do know that a canyon is coming up, and beyond that, some really big rapids. What will the rapids be like in high water, I wonder? No one even mentions them.

Once on the river the hills close in even more. At lunch we cannot even reach the banks, so we find a back eddy and crowd the boats together in quiet water beneath overhanging trees and pass lunch between the boats. Huge jungle vines hanging from the trees over our heads tempt Colorado and Celia to try Tarzan and Tarzanella acts by seeing how high they can climb up the vines hand-over-hand. Very high of course, showing off! Later we pass beneath splendid waterfalls cascading into the river's edge, and somehow we manage to catch a wild shower.

Not far ahead looms the dark maw of San José Canyon, and the flooded river pours into it, squeezing between the high walls. The loud. angry roar of the water gives us short warning of the dangers toward which we are rapidly pulled. All eyes are on the gaping chasm ahead while whirlpools—fierce, spiraling 'draw-downs' locally known as "remolinos"—are forming randomly everywhere, matched by equally random boils. The surface turbulence is overwhelming. Matt who is ahead approaching the mouth yells back "Stay off the waaaaaalls! Tamara and Doug are in the duckies. Tied with a string to Tamara's boat ahead of us is a little toy duck, that bobs merrily along beside her. With the river getting rougher and rougher, flowing faster and faster with a humpy, uneven, surface moving unpredictably, we watch as Tamara is flipped out of her boat. We freeze holding our breaths as we watch her grab the duck and then the string, thereby not losing her boat. Unbelievably she manages to struggle back in to relative safety of her ducky as we all are sucked forward between the canyon walls. An attempted rescue in this situation could have ended in a disaster. That duck and its string may have saved the lives of all of us. No time here to reflect. The mighty force of the rushing water is rapidly sweeping us directly into the wall on river right. Colorado, who is strong though small and thin, is pulling on the oars with arms that suddenly look like toothpicks and screaming, "I'm not in control!" Our raft tips dangerously beside the cliff. Charlie sitting in the bottom of the raft has turned white, yelling "high side, high side." seemingly looking at me in a moment when I've lost all sense of up and down, higher or lower, and Curt is grabbing me into the bottom of the raft. Miraculously while all this is going on, the back flow of water at the cliff's edge creates a bubbling barrier that keeps us from hitting the wall directly and we finally pull away out into the main stream.

Things are not much better in the middle of this raging torrent, but at least the big raft remains relatively level and upright. The surface is wild with remolinos and boils. The potentially lethal whirlpools come and go, and it is impossible to know where the next one will form and how to dodge it. We peer into downward spiraling vortices that are at least 15 feet deep—whirling black holes spiraling downward toward an infinity 200 feet below us. Ahead Celia's raft gets caught in a whirlpool and spirals around and around as Stephanie terrified, stares down from the high end of the tipping boat into one of these deadly open holes. Near the mouth of the canyon Matt is caught in a whirlpool weaponized with a big log that would have spelled disaster had it collided with his boat. Somehow Doug and finally Tamara manage to negotiate their way safely through this this morass of seething water, and Dan and his boat carrying Mark Michaels (and Al and Karen) slips through without a crisis. The notorious rapids at the end of the canyon were easy and 'honest' in comparison—riding the tongue of the waves, bouncing, but predictable water rollercoasters, were nothing compared with the terrorizing ferocity of the surface of Xibalba behind us.

We emerge into calm waters. Still in shock with what we've been though, we just sit there, now quietly drifting No one speaks.

Silence.

Finally Matt makes a statement, "We'll never do *that* again." While drinking Tecate with his buddies back in Palenque, had he never heard tales of running San José Canyon in high water during the rainy season? Maybe few had been so foolish. (We later learn that two weeks following our trip two guys had been sucked into a remolino in the canyon—one of them for eight minutes—and he died.)

We float into a landscape recently transformed by logging and cattle. We glide close to farms and a highway we can't see. The rain forest is mangled, broken, mutilated, open. Cows roam, and that night our so-called "cow camp" is littered with cow pies. Yes, yuk!

The next day the ever-widening, swollen river is placid. At the edge, huge orange and black iguanas rest lazily on branches above the water. We slip by quietly. Do they ever fall in, we ask ourselves. We pass the border with Guatemala and finally disembark in a small Mexican town and begin to unload the boats.

What's this dirt in my Teva—this painful, gritty nuisance under my foot hampering my steps as I carry gear from the boat up a ramp. It hurts. Where did the dirt come from in the first place? I ignore it for a while, but finally I can't stand it any longer, and examine my sandal. There is no dirt. Nothing. Why is it hurting so badly? Carla, who is a nurse, takes one look at my foot and is horrified...it's fungus *in* my foot, growing at an alarming rate, seemingly getting more invasive by the minute. Fortunately, someone has had the sense to bring anti-fungal cream on the trip. It's immediately effective, but still hobbling, back in Palenque that evening, Curt and I hire a taxi to the restaurant.

The rain forest—it'll grab ya, one way or another.

THE CHRISTMAS TREE AND OTHER THEFTS OR TRANSFORMATIONS

by

Mavis Greer

One of the most unpredictable aspects of doing archaeology as a job is when other people accompany you to the field for some aspect of a project. When this happens we have learned by experience to hope for the best but plan for the unexpected.

In the late 1970s I went to the field with oil company representatives, various well pad construction people, permit agents (those who take care of all aspects of permitting a federal well for the oil company), and the rancher. One of the permit agents (I'll call him Ray) was a good ol' boy who was quite charming and got along with most people. However, he was also one of those people who thought it was better to ask forgiveness afterwards than to ask permission beforehand.

The day started with most of us meeting at the beginning of the newly planned road along the highway north of Gillette, Wyoming. In fact, we were all there but the rancher, who was tied up and was going to catch up with us later. With so many people there were many vehicles, so we followed one another in a caravan along the two-track from the highway across the flat valley bottom into the pine and juniper covered hills. Once we arrived at the location, as we stood around waiting for the rancher to arrive, Ray decided to take a look at a different route into the well pad and off he went in his vehicle. Just about the time the rancher drove up, so did Ray. In the back of his SUV he had one of the ranchers nicest pine trees, which he had cut to bring home as his Christmas tree. While the rest of us stood there horrified, he got out of his truck with a big smile on his face so pleased with his find. The rancher was too flabbergasted to say anything at the time. Unbelievably, Ray kept his job and the well location was permitted. However, I never heard whether or not he had to pay the rancher for the tree.

More common than stealing trees is the theft of artifacts. Most of these occur at a time when the archaeologist is not there to witness it, but one nice summer day John and I met the oil company representative (I'll call him Jim) to discuss the project prior to us doing the survey. We get out of our trucks and are talking about what might be found in this area, when we look down and notice lithic artifacts at our feet. Jim reaches down and picks up a flake and proceeds to tell us how the Indians used this material to make artifacts. You know this "cal-say-donie" makes great arrowheads, he informs us. John and I are quiet and look at one another as we let him talk, but we are having a hard time controlling our laughter regarding his pronunciation of chalcedony. When he gets done telling us about lithic technology (as if we don't have a clue about it), he calmly puts the flake in his pocket and walks off.

As I mentioned, most people are not so blatant about taking artifacts from an archaeological site. Northwest of Gillette, Wyoming, we recorded a Paleoindian lithic scatter site. It is not often that we find a Goshen point on the surface, so this was a special site for us. We point plotted all the artifacts (that is, making a map from GPS measurements of where the artifacts are located on the ground) and took many photographs of the point. About two weeks later we returned to the site to take another look at the point before issuing the report. We had our site map with us and were able to walk straight to the artifact. Once there we were surprised to find a large flake at the location and not the Goshen point. We checked out all the other artifacts, and they were all there. Only the point was gone, and the thief was clever enough to replace it with another artifact but not clever enough to realize we would recognize it as a replacement. There was no way to know who was at the site between our two visits and took the point. We talked with the rancher, but he had no idea who it could have been either as too many people were in and out of that area during that time.

Sometimes encounters with artifact collectors can provide archaeologists with lithic distribution information that is completely unexpected. While in the mountains of west-central Wyoming to look at game traps one summer day, we observed collectors who had picked up several lithic artifacts as they hiked along. One woman had pulled the hem of her shirt up to form a bowl for all her artifacts at her waist as she walked. As John and I sat on a rock resting near one of the game traps she comes up to talk. As she stands there she decides she is tired of carrying these artifacts and dumps them in a pile near her feet. Now, archaeologists are familiar with what are termed "collector piles" on sites, but it is usually assumed that they came from the site on which they are found, but this shows us that it not always the case.

ALTARES AND THE RAID ON SANTA ELENA
by
POLLY SCHAAFSMA

"Y'all come on down," they said. It was mid-April, 1987.

It is an enticing invitation from our friends, Tom and Betty Alex in Big Bend National Park. We always like a little trip south at the end of winter as a relief from the endless cold winds and tan monotony of early spring in northern New Mexico. Tom and Betty have recently met Alberto Silva from Santa Elena, a little border farming community in Chihuahua, across from Castolon, and he has offered to take us in his truck to a petroglyph site at some distance from his village. And we can make prior arrangements to have a good Mexican meal at the mayor's house at the end of the day. Enedina Ortega, the mayor's wife, has a little two-table patio business making meals for the occasional adventurous tourist or other wayfarers who manage to find their way into this isolated spot. Of course we are intrigued. Finding the whole idea very attractive, we are soon packed and heading south on the 10 hour drive to the park.

Several miles below the mouth of Santa Elena Canyon on the Mexican border, and across the Rio Grande, sits Santa Elena ("Sanaleena" in local gringo lingo). Here rows of adobe houses line up along peaceful, dusty streets shaded by a few cottonwoods. On approach from the American side, the town is hidden above by the tall banks of the Rio Grande crowded with mesquite thickets and tall stands of cane grasses. Enedina's oldest son runs a little enterprise of his own shuttling people across the river in a small row boat for a few pesos. Once across the unmarked border, a climb up the sandy bluff along a well-worn path takes us quickly to the straight dirt streets of the *ejido* community, where we are met by our host. Following introductions and other pleasantries, we climb into Alberto's truck and are off.

It's a fair distance to our destination, a place called Altares. We wind and bounce over rough ranch roads through an arid landscape splashed by the pale greenery of sotol, lecheguilla and prickly pear amidst finely textured creosote bushes dotted with yellow flowers. Every plant seems 'arranged' or placed in perfect harmony with the landscape across gravely desert pavement, like a well-kept garden. We eventually arrive at the head of a little canyon where a flat sandy corridor runs between looming, dark gray rock walls carved with petroglyphs.

Small images of ancient Shumla projectile points, unrecognizable life forms, some human, and a rabbit perhaps, reveal the ancient presence of early foragers. A bow and arrow hunter, dressed as an Apache, and rancher's names are further testimony to a continued human activity over centuries through this magical passageway. It is a lovely day in the Chihuahua desert, serene, quiet and warm—paradisal relief from the stark north where we live. After using up all our film—this was prior to the days of digital photography—we climb back into the truck and return to Santa Elena. Enedina's cozy dining room and her delicious beans and tacos are a satisfying finale to a perfect day.

Back in Santa Fe, eight days later, we hear of a violent raid that is making international news. But without TV, and before the internet, we can't find out much about it, except that the Mexican government invaded Santa Elena with helicopters and gunned down some drug dealer. It was kind of scary, even unbelievable to think we'd walked through this remote peaceful settlement just a week before. What about Alberto? Enedina and her sons? Are they okay?

Mexico—well, you never know.

Years go by, and the raid on Santa Elena becomes just one more of the many news items of drug-related violence filtering north from the border.

In 2001 we attend an Old-Timer's reunion in Big Bend National Park. Curt had spent summers there with his park ranger Dad when he was a kid, and he wants to reconnect with some of his old friends and acquaintances. In a hall filled with old park service folks and West Texas ranchers, there are speeches and presentations of recollections, mostly of "the good old days" when sheep ranching was allowed, rampant and unchecked, destroying most of the desert's vegetation. To us it was disappointing that little was said about the Park itself, finally restored to its natural balance resulting in the beautiful place that it is today. The organizers hand out raffle tickets at the door and during the program, to relieve any potential boredom (and maintain the attendance), they stop the show once in a while and call out winning numbers. Almost half the people in the audience win something this afternoon—items from the Park Service gift shop, mostly books of which there is an endless variety. There are books on Big Bend geology, Big Bend flowers, Big Bend cactus, Big Bend birds. The books include essays on Big Bend history, Big Bend legends, adventurers in Big Bend, and all kinds of things about the Big Bend ranchers, miners, and others who had once lived there and had exploited, protected or simply enjoyed it. And let's not forget the big picture books of colored photographs of Big Bend scenery.

Then they call out my number.

I get up and walk to the front expectantly to collect my prize. I have never won anything. They hand me a rather garish, thick, paperback with red, white, and green stripes on the cover superimposed by a black and white photo of a tough looking desperado with a sideways glance. The title printed in bold black letters is "Drug Lord." I am so embarrassed. While making my way to my seat in the back of the room, passing been the rows of staunchly conservative Anglo ranchers and park people, I sort of hide the book under my arm, hoping no one will look or remember the title the master-of ceremonies called out as he handed it to me. I feel contaminated. And even cheated. The park book store must have just wanted to get rid of it. What was a book like that doing the Big Bend book shop?

Eventually—maybe within an hour or two—curiousity gets the better of me, and I open it up. As I scan through a few pages, I realize it is very well written. Hmmm. I become even more curious—it is about drug-running along the border in the Big Bend country. With a little more scrutiny, it becomes clear that the focus is on Santa Elena and the events leading up to the 'mysterious' raid on the village just eight days following our visit there fourteen years earlier. The pages describe in detail how they caught this guy—this drug lord, Pablo Acosta, featured on the cover—who had had a huge 'plaza'—a drug operation with the protection of the Mexican government, in exchange for enormous payoffs. Importing cocaine from Colombia to Ojinaga was one of his most profitable enterprises, supplemented by trafficking marijuana. The book explains, too, how the Mexican government would even destroy his competitors, in order to maintain Pablo's lucrative income and thus the big payments from him flowing into Mexico City. After years of this, however, he was going downhill in health and reliability, himself an addict and sick, and with their own interests in mind, the government wanted him gone...and, of course, replaced.

Pablo was a native of Santa Elena. He felt safe there in his house with two-foot thick mud walls and fortified windows and doors. In the spring of 1987, ill, weak, and in hiding he took refuge in his old home, knowing they were after him. The climax of the book was the raid. At the time we were there, complex plans were already in the works on both sides of border for taking him out, a plot as yet undisclosed to the park rangers. In the book, author Terrence Poppa, recounts the attack in vivid detail. He describes the terror of Enedina and her children as a gunman invaded her house and ordered everyone down, while outside helicopters swept close and roared overhead and the sound of machine gun fire ripped through the village. Pablo's roof was set on fire, and a fierce gun battle ensued, finally killing him. Miraculously, Pablo was the only person that died in that operation. His place was just three houses away from Enedina's.

Yes, Mexico can be little dicey. Now we know that story.

SQUEEZING THROUGH SMALL PLACES AND HANGING OFF HIGH CLIFFS

by

MAVIS GREER

If you do rock art archaeology, you will sometimes (probably more than you'd like) find yourself either squeezing through a small cave passage or climbing a high cliff to see a site that you absolutely cannot live without. That's certainly been the case for me more times I than I can probably remember. However, there are a few times that stand out in my mind.

I've never been a caver, but John was a caver from a young age and loves the dark zones of long, deep caves. I, on the other hand, only want to venture that far back into a completely dark tunnel if there is a good archaeological site at the end of the trip. In 1991 we spent some time in Guatemala working for Dr. Jim Brady, who is known for his cave archaeology studies. One day John and I, along with Brian, who was 11 years old at the time, joined Jim's team to visit a Mayan cave with many archaeological remains. While John went with a group to look at a burial, Brian and I stayed with Jim to go look at a ritual room with paintings and a carved chair, used as a throne. After walking through the cave entrance we took off down a passage that became increasingly narrower until we were crawling on our hands and knees. I was following some caver archaeologists, and I was followed by Brian and then Jim, who was bringing up the rear. Brian became increasingly worried we would get stuck since the passage kept getting smaller, but Jim assured him it would be fine as "we sent your Mom in first, so if she gets stuck, we know we need to back out."

Well, we all made it through the passage, which it turned out was much bigger than the next place we had to negotiate. Just prior to getting into the ritual room, the passage closed off, and you made a choice to climb up a steep wall and go through a fairly large hole or to get on your stomach and slither through a narrow crack with the cave pressing you on the back and stomach. Not being a climber, I opted for the stomach crawl with one other girl, while everyone else (including Brian) climbed the wall to the larger hole. Once I started the stomach crawl behind the younger, skinner, girl, I started to doubt I had made the right decision. I'm somewhat claustrophobic anyway, and this confirmed I was worse than I thought. It was impossible to raise your head, which had to be level with your back, and slithering along for about 15 feet challenged me to my limit. I was never so happy to see the big room on the other side. The ritual room was spectacular and a vision I still hold in my mind. The carved throne, the many offerings of pottery and other items, and the rock art covering the walls of this dark-zone room was something not many people will ever be able to see, and it was worth my discomfort to see it. When it came time to leave, I still couldn't find the courage to make the climb, so once again I chose the slithering route, which had not improved since I arrived.

In southeastern New Mexico is Surratt Cave, another place of rituals with many pictographs and another narrow squeeze. I've been to this cave more than once, but only once have I ventured into it. Even then it took me two days to decide that I could make it. The cave entrance is within a rocky breakdown area in bowl-like sink within the piñon pine area of the state. Even the entrance to the squeeze is small as shown on the introductory photo to this chapter. Once you drop into that entrance hole you have to crawl through a narrow passage with a ninety-degree turn just before reaching a small squeeze hole, which John is looking out of in the photo included with this chapter, to enter the main cave. Having navigated the crawl part of the entrance my first time in the cave, I balked at going through that squeeze hole feeling confident I would get stuck! John proceeded through and spent the day taking photographs and notes on the rock art. The next day he talked me into trying again and assured me that I could make it through. After putting on a pair of tights (rather than jeans), my thinnest T-shirt, and a pair of tennis shoes rather than boots, I was ready to give it a try. John went in first to guide me down as once through the hole, which you have to enter feet first, you have to make contact with a small foot hold before reaching the floor of the room. I finally gathered up my courage to give it a try, and with John talking me through, I was able to hold my breathe and get through the small squeeze hole and into the first room, which seemed big after the hole, but was really not much bigger than a standard kitchen. I felt so happy to have gotten to that point that I pretty much forgot that I would have to leave the cave the same way I entered. However, first I had to leave the small room, and to do that we made a crawl through a small passage that was not as tight as the one in the Guatemalan cave, but this one was full of stickers. Finally in the larger main room, I was happy that John had come into it earlier that morning and placed lights around it so I could get a good view of the cave and feel comfortable about the rest of the adventure. We then spent the day looking at the rock art in several rooms, including a narrow crack that has a large painted cloud terrace on one wall. When the day ended and I again approached the entrance hole, my anxiety level again began to rise. However, just like a horse heading for the barn, I stepped up on the foot hole, put my arms over my head and through the hole, pulled myself up through the hole, navigated the narrow entrance, and never looked back being so happy to see the outside world.

The next time I visited that cave I thought I could go in without any trauma having done it before, but once I arrived at the narrow squeeze hole I couldn't believe how small it was and wondered how I ever made it through there the first time. I quickly decided I'd been there and done that and didn't need to do it again.

In central Montana along the Smith River is Dillinger Cave, which is really just an enlarged rockshelter room. It lies high on the mountainside overlooking the Smith River valley. In the summer of 1992 we obtained permission of the landowner to visit the cave and do some recording. The hike to the cave begins behind their cabin, and it's a relatively steep climb up the mountainside for a nearly 200 feet vertical gain through the forest. However, that portion of the access was the easiest part. Just below the cave mouth is a 30-foot vertical rough limestone outcropping. I took one look at that rocky wall and decided there is no way I'm making it into that cave. Well, John and Brian climbed the wall easily finding hand and foot holds that they felt comfortable with but realized I would never do it without something sturdier to hold onto, so they strung a rope for me. However, the rope didn't do much to assuage my fears as I looked down the steep, long slope to the river and imagined falling all that distance. But John convinced me I could make the climb, so up I went with him behind me telling me where to step. I finally made it into the room, and the pictographs in the room made the scariness of the climb all worth it, although I was convinced I would never leave the cave. In fact, I told them just to wave when they passed by in the future as I wasn't coming down. However, after a few hours in the cave, I knew this wasn't the home for me, and John, with the help of the rope, was able to talk me out of the cave.

I really thought I wouldn't encounter a scarier climb than Dillinger Cave, but this was not to be. A few years later in 2001 we accompanied a group of cavers to Frozen Leg Cave above the Bighorn River in southeastern Montana. This is really a cave system, with the cave on the right having long passages with no archaeology and the cave on the left having a few rooms filled with rock art. I had wanted to see these paintings for a long time, so I was excited to have the opportunity to visit the site, which is on private land.

We parked our vehicles on the high crest of the rim above the canyon walls and began the steep walk down the slope. Upon reaching the level of the cave entrances, we cut across from the trail over to the base of the limestone cliff below the holes in the wall. Although the open cliff face below the cave entrance is not a long climb, it is steep, slippery, and drops down to the river several hundred feet below, so sometime in the past someone anchored an iron chain caving ladder to the limestone wall to help people make the climb. I took one look at that ladder and decided I wasn't going to see the paintings after all. However, John tried out the ladder, decided it was safe, and came back down to help me up to the top. After much cajoling on his part and much whining on mine, I finally agreed to give it a try. He kept telling me not to look down, but I couldn't help but look at my feet a couple of times and was petrified by what I saw below. It was several hundred feet to the reservoir below, and that drop included numerous cliffs with some narrow benches that weren't wide enough for me to balance on and were sloping. At that point though I had to push forward and finally made it to the top but then had to sit at the entrance and let my heart return to normal beating before checking out the rock art.

I'm happy to report the pictographs lived up to their expectations, and it was definitely worth the climb. However, when it came time to go back down that ladder, I was again having second (or third or more) thoughts about why I'd come into the cave. Luckily, John was again able to talk me down the ladder. Since then the ladder has been removed due to safely concerns, but this is another place I've labeled, been there, done that.

So, thinking of doing some archaeological site visiting or recording? Hope you are not afraid of heights or claustrophobic as you will have to deal with both in your career.

EASTER SUNDAY DELIVERY
by
Polly Schaafsma

"Let's go to Jaguar Cave," I suggest. It is an Easter morning in the late 1970s, and we are driving back to New Mexico, following a family visit in Fort Davis, Texas. Off to an early start, we have time for a little side-trip to Jaguar Cave in the Chihuahuan desert north of the Rio Grande. The black soot-covered ceiling has white paintings of a great horned serpent, a bear and other animals. One with spots suggests a jaguar and thus the name. We have been there before, but somehow without any photographic equipment. Today we have a camera with us, and that, combined with the fact that there is no rush to get anywhere in particular, we can drive out there and take a few photographs at leisure.

We turn off the main highway paralleling the Mexican border around Fort Hancock, and follow a broad ranch road north. White and well-graded, it curves gently over and around limestone swells and crosses empty creosote flats that extend for miles. In the distance low mountains rise. Lonely country. There is no one else out here, and we joke that everyone in the region is happily at the dining room table over-indulging in an Easter dinner.

After a long drive, we recognize a small road to the right that will take us further into the back country until we reach a dam across a dry wash where water pools following summer thunderstorms. Our route is marked by low dips where stands of mesquite and other tall vegetation, break the monotony of the creosote. The turn off the main ranch road heads directly into one of these thickets. As we make the sharp corner onto the small track we are startled to find a small plane parked right in the middle of the road blocking our route. The plane is well hidden from every direction, obviously having been backed into this brushy spot, and conveniently facing a long stretch of straight road—an opportune runway.

Drug dealers! I freak out.

Curt, at the wheel and thinking only in terms of the logistics of maneuvering around the plane and without considering who had parked it, calmly says, "I wonder if we can make it under the wing." We are driving a little Honda Civic, and although it is low enough to scoot past, Curt is also concerned that someone might be in the cockpit and start the propellers.

We forge ahead under the left wing with space to spare. The cockpit is empty as far as I can tell.

As we speed ahead, in the rearview mirror Curt sees a van approaching the plane, and he comments that it is too high to follow our act. "For Good God's sake", I scream, "What are you thinking? They *don't want* to get under the wing. They're bringing the pilot back after loading the loot into the van." Keeping an eye on the events taking place behind us, we race away down the flat, straight road—soon-to-be-runway—ahead, and within three minutes the plane is in the air and gone. Our minds also race with the "What ifs... what if our vehicle had been too high to make it under the wing and the van had driven up, trapping us between the van and the plane?

What if we had arrived at the scene a little sooner when they were in the act of returning the pilot to the plane, blocking the road? Would they have shot us? No one would have ever known what had happened. No one knew we were out there.

And yes, we did get our photographs at the cave.

Mavis in the open country planned for drilling on the Crow Reservation.
(Photograph by John Greer)

The Rio Usumacinta in flood, October 1992. (Photograph by Curt Schaafsma)

Entrance to Yaxchilan. (Photograph by Polly Schaafsma)

Plaza in Yaxchilan.
(Photograph by Polly Schaafsma)

Lacandon rain forest resident.
(Photograph by Karen Hayes, courtesy of Polly Schaafsma)

Curtis in rubber ducky. (Photograph by Karen Hayes, courtesy of Polly Schaafsma)

"Money face", Maya architecture visible through the vegetation at the site of Piedras Negras, Guatemala. (Photograph by Polly Schaafsma)

Resting along the Usumacinta: lunch time entertainment by Red Wolf.
(Photograph by Karen Hayes, courtesy of Polly Schaafsma)

Taking showers along the way.
(Photograph by Karen Hayes, courtesy
of Polly Schaafsma)

Wide, placid waters of the Usumacinta.
(Photograph by Curt Schaafsma)

Trees and sandstone northwest of Gillette, Wyoming.
(Photograph by John Greer)

Chalcedony: This material is highly variable but usually semi-translucent whitish (like chert) to an almost agate-like appearance. It also is based in quartz and has a somewhat waxy luster with a range in colors from white to gray, grayish-blue, and brown to nearly black.

Arrowpoint and scraper from northeastern Wyoming.
(Photograph by John Greer)

Discarded collector's pile of artifacts. (Photograph by John Greer)

Rio Grande near Santa Elena. (Photograph by Curt Schaafsma)

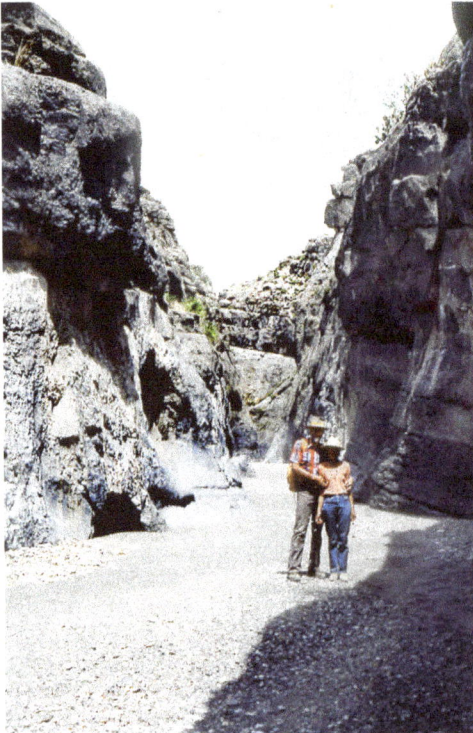

Curt and Polly in the canyon near Altares, Chihuahua.
(Photograph by Tom Alex)

Petroglyphs and modern graffiti in the canyon.
(Photograph by Polly Schaafsma)

Drug Lord! (Photograph by Curtis Schaafsma)

John looking back at me after having gone through the small squeeze at the end of the entrance crawl in Surratt Cave, New Mexico, that must be negotiated before entering the cave proper. (Photograph by Mavis Greer)

John in the narrow, lower room of Surratt Cave, New Mexico. (Photograph by Mavis Greer)

Looking out the mouth of Dillinger Cave (24CA346) in central Montana. Mavis is the blue spot to the left on the platform trying to gain courage to go up the rocky climb into the painted shelter. (Photograph by John Greer)

Frozen Leg Cave (24BH425), southern Montana. Arrow points to the location of the old metal caving ladder. (Photograph by John Greer)

Looking out of Frozen Leg Cave, southern Montana from the safe interior. (Photograph by John Greer)

Visitors at Jaguar Cave in 1995. Identifiable are Polly (second from left),
Scotty MacNeish (center), and Francisco Mendiola (right).
(Photograph by Curt Schaafsma)

Large painting of a bear in Jaguar Cave. It is worth pointing out that among the many
animals represented, there is no clear representation of a jaguar.
(Photograph by Curt Schaafsma)

7
FUN WITH THE MEDIA

Rock Art brings out reporters. Cover of The Montana Pioneer, August 2002.

FIFTEEN MINUTES OF FAME
by
Mavis Greer

In early spring of 2016 I received a call from Macie, who owns the Bear Gulch Pictographs and has been talked about elsewhere in these stories. She had exciting news. While watching a TV show on unusual things that people had inherited her son Ray said, "hey, we should be on that show. We inherited a rock art site." Macie agreed, and they contacted the producers about doing a show on the Bear Gulch Pictographs. Macie was calling to see if I would vouch for them as the producers wanted to make sure it really was an inheritance and worthy of a show. I was more than happy to do so.

In May 2016 the producer (I'll call her Jenny) called and we had a long talk about the site, how Macie and Ray came to own it, and the importance of it. The show was more than interested, and they were ready to set up filming in early June. Although originally I was only supposed to vouch for the site, during my talk with Jenny I agreed to come and talk about the site as part of the show. She asked for both John and me to do it, and I agreed for both of us, but John was reluctant, so I ended up doing it myself while he watched.

It was all set for June 8th, and we were sent the details regarding the schedule, which was to be a short morning interview. About this same time I began corresponding with the field producer for the show, whom I'll call Leslie. She put me on the schedule for ten o'clock in the morning and gave instructions about what to wear: sensible shoes as we would be walking along the cliff face, solid colors (avoid white, black, polka dots, stripes or checks), and no logos, denim, or khaki. We were then invited to join the cast and crew for lunch after the shoot. We also had nondisclosure forms to complete that didn't allow us to share the details of the program on social media before it aired.

This all sounded short, sweet, and well organized. We planned to head to Montana the night before, spend the night with Macie and her husband Dan, and head home as soon the filming was done that day. Well, the best laid plans, etc. It wasn't long before that schedule was history, but we had already arrived at Macie's house before we received a new one that had us on at 3:30 p.m. The revised schedule was very detailed with what was happening when down to makeup touchups and tweaking any needed lights. However, soon this schedule was also thrown out the window.

The morning of June 8th arrived, and we all drove the 30 miles or so from Macie's house to the site. A group of people that had been hand-picked to take a tour of the site that was to be filmed for the show were there and ready for Ray to guide them through the site with the film crew. We waited in the picnic area in the trees by the small Bear Gulch stream so as not to interfere and chatted while waiting for the next step.

Jenny was not there yet, but soon Sharon (the gopher for the production) received a call from her that she was in Lewistown at the hotel. She was staying at a historic hotel and was given a room on the second floor. There was no elevator, so she wasn't sure how she was going to get her luggage into the room; obviously carrying it herself was not an option. She wanted Sharon to come back to town (about a half hour drive) and take her luggage up to the room; evidently there was no one at the hotel who wanted to help an able-bodied, young, athletic-looking woman. In the meantime, Sharon was supposed to deliver Macie to a nearby country bed and breakfast where the crew was staying so that she could meet Jenny for a sit-down interview, and then she was to pick up the lunches from a sandwich place in town. She managed to do it all: I went with Macie to the B&B (she took both of us in her small personal car), and then she went to Lewistown for lunch and to move luggage. John and Dan (Macie's husband) accompanied her to Lewistown for the lunch pickup, but someone from the hotel had already moved Jenny's luggage by the time they got there.

The shoot with Macie was indoors in a living room of the B&B. It was interesting in that Jenny wanted Macie to play up that she didn't have any money to run the site because people often wanted to donate to the cause. Both of us were uncomfortable with that angle, but Jenny assured us that it was something acceptable for the program. The interview took about an hour and then Sharon showed up with sandwiches for us for lunch. We ate outside on the patio with Jenny and a few of the crew, including her makeup person. All was going well until Jenny thought a bee was in her hair. After a big show of brushing it away, she moved indoors. The B&B was beautiful, inside and out. Set in the foothills of the Snowy Mountains, the scenery was great, and the wood-themed interior was welcoming and upscale. Undoubtedly the old hotel could not hold a candle to this new B&B, which I'm sure was disconcerting to Jenny who was stuck at the hotel.

Some time after lunch we finally left for the site again. We again road with Sharon, who entertained us with accounts of her adventures working as a gopher for film crews that came to Montana. We had never heard of such a job before, and decided it was probably not for us since she was at the beck and call of a bunch of divas from what we gathered. Arriving at the site, we found they were not ready for us yet.

After waiting around as people came and went setting up lights and sound systems, near 5 pm they were ready to interview me. Jenny and I were to sit at a picnic table they had moved over into the grassy, Bear Gulch creek valley bottom below the cliff. We were across the table from one another, and after they had affixed microphones to us, she began to ask me questions. However, we had barely begun when the camera crew decided they could not see enough of my face because of my hair. They sent Jenny's makeup person over to see if she could do something with my hair. She decided I was a hopeless case letting me know that I simply had "too much hair." However, they finally did get it pulled back they way they wanted it. We then proceeded with the interview. The early evening weather was fantastic...it was sunny, calm, and miraculously there were hardly any bugs. However, it wasn't long before a hair came across Jenny's face. It was a single hair and not noticeable to anyone but her, but she stopped everything and called her makeup person over to get it off her face. The rest of us were wondering why her hand could not reach up and brush it away.

As we neared the end of the interview at the picnic table, I remembered I said something about ASM dating, but I couldn't remember if I said ASM or MAS. I was horrified and asked Jenny if we could redo that part. She responded that it was not necessary as they wouldn't use that as she couldn't figure out what I was talking about. Too bad, documentation on how old the site is seemed like an important thing to tell the public to me.

Leaving the table we moved up to the cliff face with the camera and sound people. As we walked along the cliff we talked about various images. It seemed to be going well, and I guess it was as Jenny complimented me with "good transition" as we moved from one image to the next. It was nearly dark when we finished along the cliff. At that point Jenny wanted pictures of herself with the crew and Macie along the cliff, so I became the photographer and took pictures of the group on Jenny's iPhone.

Before leaving the cliff, the camera man said he needed a portrait photo of me. I haven't been photogenic since I was four, so I wasn't looking forward to this part. However, the camera man was great. He took photos, showed them to me, and then reshot them until I said okay, that's acceptable.

By then it was dark, and Dan and Macie had a big fire going in a pit down by the picnic tables. They had brought hot dogs and hamburgers into the canyon for a party at the end of the filming day. It was great food, and even Jenny, who looked like she ate nothing but a lettuce leaf now and then, was spotted eating a hot dog.

Once the show made it to the editing phase, we thought they were done with us, but they then needed photos of us from the past at the site. We found several, and so John made it onto the show through those even though he passed on being in on the filming. They also did some fact checking of statements they were going to make in voice overs; this really impressed me that they were concerned that they wouldn't be perpetuating crazy information as is often done by the media for rock art (and other archaeological) sites, such as demonstrated in the "Taken for a Ride In Baja" story that follows.

TAKEN FOR A RIDE
by
POLLY SCHAAFSMA

I really wanted to go to Baja California and see the Great Murals. We had recently been introduced to them through copious photographs and a video by Harry Crosby and Enrique Hambleton. These adventurers had visited hundreds of these paintings in central Baja California, as they rode mules up the Camino Real following the old Spanish mission trail from Loreto to northern California. In his writings and conversations, Crosby conveyed his enthusiasm for the people who lived in these remote sierras. The ranchers encountered along the way had been eager to show "Los Dos Enriques" the cave paintings in their areas, and in the course of their expeditions, they had photographed hundreds of sites that until that time were pretty much unknown to archaeologists, who were aware of only a handful that had been recently published: (Earle S. Gardner, *The Hidden Heart of Baja*, 1962; Clement Meighan, "Prehistoric Rock Painting in Baja California." *American Antiquity,* 1966, and *Indian Art and History: The Testimony of Prehispanic Rock Paintings in Baja California*. 1969; and Campbell Grant, *Rock Art of Baja California,* 1974).

Crosby was also captivated by the exotic desert environment populated with an endless parade of strange plants—the huge cardones, torotes, ocotillo, ironwoods, mesquites, the bizarre zalate, several varieties of the palo verde, palo blanco, and the famous pitaya dulce, a columnar cactus known for its delicious fruit. Desert rats ourselves, we were immediately intrigued by the whole package and hoped to get there someday. Rock art tourism had not yet hit the sierras.

Early one morning in May of 1977, as the sun is just barely beaming above the Sangre de Cristo Mountains and we are still in bed, we reluctantly answer the ringing phone. Very quickly I notice that Curt is very involved in an animated conversation that begins to sound like a plot or invitation of some kind to go on a rock art trip—to the Four Corners, perhaps?—Or wherever. I am interested.

He hangs up. Plans seem to have been made or at least responded to in a positive way.

"Who was that?"

"*The Republic Investigator*."

I have heard of them. A dignified name, some reliable outfit possibly—a newspaper? "They want to take us to Baja?"

"What do you think of that?"

"How come? Why do they want to take us to Baja—all expenses paid, a nice honorarium. Everything. Wow! Why?"

"They want us to give them background on the murals."

[Well, you have to understand that back in those days, we were living in a small village in northern New Mexico and fleeing the world. We did not watch TV, nor did we read newspapers, and we were not familiar with any of the latter. To us, *The Investigator* was comparable, perhaps, to the *New York Times*. We'd heard of both, and we knew nothing.]

Fair enough, perhaps, we are thinking. It sounds as if they want to write an informative piece with photos, supported by archaeological information. Sounds okay. The general public is increasingly interested in rock art. Perhaps *The Investigator* has a scientific section.

But there's one thing already on the side of caution—they have seen pictures from Cueva San Borjitas and the human-like figures there seem to be flying. Some seem to wear space suits. These journalists think that perhaps they depict space aliens and that these pictures have been well hidden all this time in the remote galleries of the Baja California sierras. Well, this is crazy, but of course we'll straighten them out. Actually, they *need* us—so we think.

At last! We are going to Baja. Plans are finalized. We will fly to San Diego where we will join up with the paper's journalist and photographer, proceed from there in a small plane to the remote landing strip near San Ignacio, a tiny mission village in the middle of the peninsula.

We meet as planned—these two Brits—jolly, boisterous fellows they are with grand enthusiasm for everything. First, we need to shop, since it is up to us to provide food for the expedition into the mountains. Their exuberance extends to the multitude of food options in powdery form billed as 'camp food'— powdered eggs, powdered milk, dried stew and so forth. Advertised as delicious and obviously light to carry, powdered and dried grub will make life easier for the burros we will hire to carry our gear. In our wanderings through the supermarket, however, Curt grabs a big container of instant oatmeal, just in case the local guides do not have a taste for powdered fare. And the Brits themselves, go on a search for Kendall Mint Cake, a thick, sugary candy bar with a strong mint flavor, popular in England, and which they cannot, it seems, live without. I'd never heard of it, but miraculously they find it and purchase a good supply calculated to last through our travels.

Once the supplies are in hand, we go to the airport and load everything into the small plane and head south. This is not what one might call a luxury aircraft. It is sparsely furnished inside. As it lumbers slowly across the skies toward San Ignacio, I am becoming increasingly uncomfortable. I have to pee in the worst way. What can I possibly do up here in mid air. Finally in desperation I mention this to the pilot, who comes up with a simple solution. "There's a tin can in back of the seats you can use." Good god! In this tiny plane with four guys. Nevertheless, it works.

On our arrival above San Ignacio, the pilot flies low, buzzing the local hotel, a signal for them to send a taxi to pick us up at the airstrip isolated in the desert several miles away. Each step toward reaching the sierras, getting on a mule and on the trail to the caves without any prior planning, goes smoothly without a hitch because folks in Mexico know how to make things work at a moment's notice, and we are soon creeping and bumping in a taxi over a most inconceivably rocky road toward Rancho Santa Marta. Situated in wide valley in the heart of the Sierra de San Francisco, in 1977 this is only road into the sierra. Other sierra ranches are accessible only by mule. En route, at Crosby's suggestion, we also visit Tacho Arce at Rancho Esperanza, who will guide us and will bring the needed mules and burros to Santa Marta for the trip.

We spend the night camped near the ranch. Proudly, the next morning the Brits display their skills at cooking powdered eggs. No one is impressed. The Mexican guys refuse to eat it. The local men, our guides, make sure that the women of their households supply them ample back-up for the trip in the form of stacks of flour tortillas, their homemade delicious goat cheese, and local dates. They also quickly embraced the *avena* (oatmeal) that Curt had made sure was purchased.

Finally mounted on our mules, we head into the mountains. The trails are rough, rocky, and steep, and only mules and burros can safely negotiate them. They take us to more remote ranches, among them a watery canyon Shangri-la where citrus, mangos, and vegetable gardens abound, fed by water from desert springs. On our approach to this ranch we meet the elderly proprietors, Loreto Arce accompanied by his wife Doña Josefa, who is comfortably riding side-saddle over this steep terrain. A snapshot of the eighteenth century. Along the way we stop at numerous open rock shelters (usually referred to as caves) to photograph the large murals. In black and red, panoramas of life-size men and women standing in static frontal poses in the midst sierra and ocean fauna grace these walls. Deer, bighorn sheep, mountain lions, rabbits, and large birds—possibly condors—along with sea lions, turtles, manta rays and fish move beneath among and over the human figures.

Curt and I are enchanted.

The Brits, not so much. The people facing us in these murals are explicitly human beings. They are not even abstractions but they are naturalistic. None of them looks like a space alien. None wears a "space suit." And in our conversations, we are not twisting facts to satisfy the goals of our new-found "friends" for a sensational newspaper article. In fact, the Brits are becoming aggravated with us. And we don't give an inch. They make remarks between themselves as to the non-cooperation of the scientists they commonly and unwittingly hire to support a sensational fantasy. They are no longer jovial. They become downright grouchy.

We don't care.

Finally, we are standing in front of the grand murals at Cueva Pintada in Arroyo San Pablo. Animals sweep the rock scape, and among them, the painted people stand like frozen sentinels. Alas, in the midst of the overlays and underlays, the Brits seize upon a small sketch in black—a poorly defined figure that they decide will serve their needs—a sketchy drawing of a 'space ship'—or so they will claim.

We're done. Climbing out of his deep canyon, we reach the then isolated rancho of San Francisco high in the sierra. At the top of the trail to Santa Marta there is a shrine where one can leave offerings for the saint's blessings and protection during the hazardous descent to where our trip began.

An article was eventually published and they used our names to support their claims. We were horrified and embarrassed to have been so naïve and foolish as to have been tricked into this. It wasn't long before the director of a prestigious Santa Fe institution and our employer at the time, called us up, wanting to know what was going on. A major donor had seen our names in the article. We were a disgrace to the organization. We explained, apologized, and fortunately for us, all was forgiven and that was the end of the issue.

We had learned a lot about tabloid newspapers and "how things work."

Archaeologists beware.

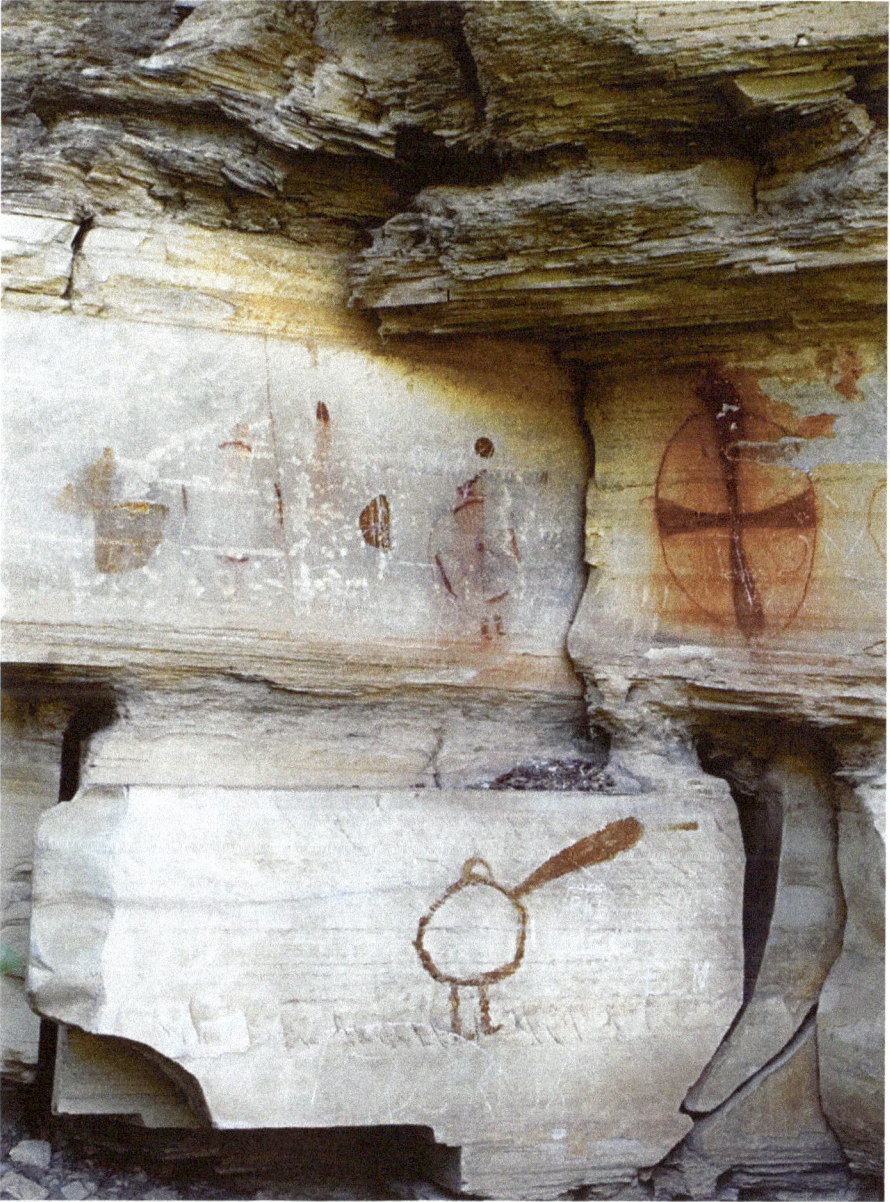

Paintings of shields and shield-bearers at Bear Gulch (24FR2), Montana. (Photograph by Mavis Greer)

Setting up to interview Mavis in the pasture below the Bear Gulch site.
(Photograph by John Greer)

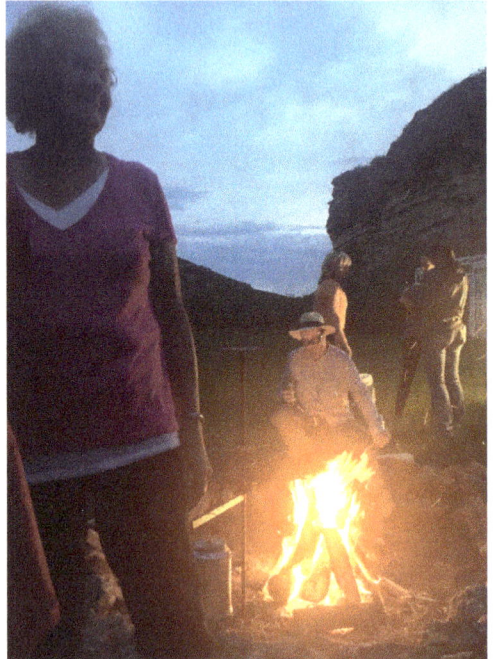

Party after the shoot in the pasture
below the Bear Gulch site.
(Photograph by Mavis Greer)

A goat ranch in the Baja sierras. (Photograph by Curt Schaafsma)

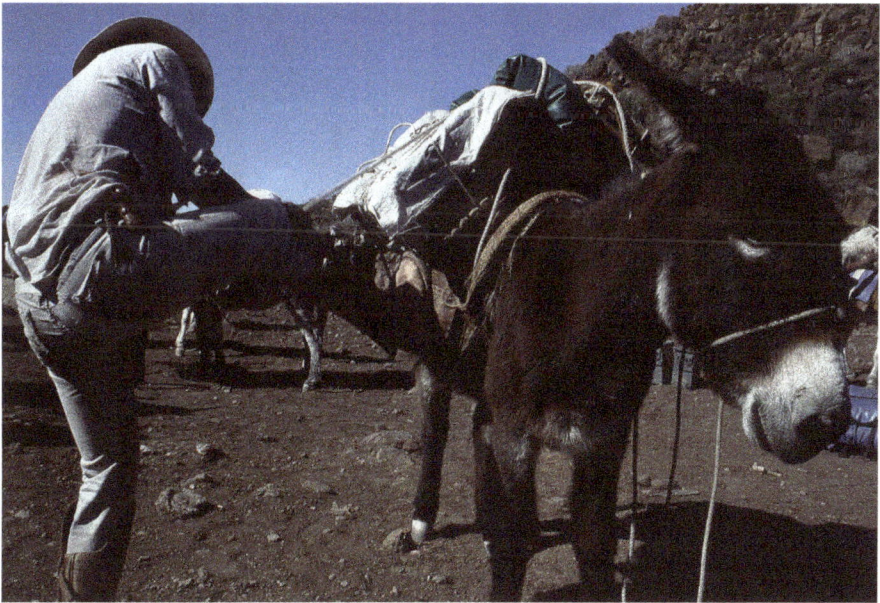

Oscar Arce, packing a burro. (Photograph by Polly Schaafsma)

Our guides from the Sierra de San Francisco
(from left to right: Sylvestre, Francisco, and Oscar Arce, and unknown).
(Photograph by Polly Schaafsma)

A sierra trail so steep we had to dismount. (Photograph by Polly Schaafsma)

Paintings in Cueva Pintada. (Photograph by Polly Schaafsma)

Close-up of paintings in Cueva Pintada. (Photograph by Polly Schaafsma)

Satisfactory object of the quest: A sketchy figure in black misinterpreted as a space ship. (Photograph by Curt Schaafsma)